W9-AXY-800

WITHDRAWN

Fidel Castro

by Michael V. Uschan

LUCENT BOOKS
A part of Gale, Cengage Learning

GALE
CENGAGE Learning™

Detroit • New York • San Francisco • New Haven, Conn • Waterville, Maine • London

LIBRARY OF CONGRESS CATALOGING-IN-PUBLICATION DATA

Uschan, Michael V., 1948-
Fidel Castro / by Michael V. Uschan.
    p. cm. -- (People in the news)
Includes bibliographical references and index.
ISBN 978-1-4205-0059-2 (hardcover)
1. Castro, Fidel, 1926---Juvenile literature. 2. Cuba--History--1959-1990--Juvenile literature. 3. Cuba--History--1933-1959--Juvenile literature. 4. Cuba--History--1990-- Juvenile literature. 5. Heads of state--Cuba--Biography--Juvenile literature. 6. Revolutionaries--Cuba--Biography--Juvenile literature. I. Title.
F1788.22.C3U83 2008
972.9106'4092--dc22
[B]
                                                                        2008029895

Lucent Books
27500 Drake Rd
Farmington Hills MI 48331

ISBN-13: 978-1-4205-0059-2
ISBN-10: 1-4205-0059-7

Dedication
Yo soy dedicado esto libro con amor a Mark Bates—Tio.

Printed in the United States of America
1 2 3 4 5 6 7 12 11 10 09 08

Contents

Fame and celebrity are alluring. People are drawn to those who walk in fame's spotlight, whether they are known for great accomplishments or for notorious deeds. The lives of the famous pique public interest and attract attention, perhaps because their experiences seem in some ways so different from, yet in other ways so similar to, our own.

Newspapers, magazines, and television regularly capitalize on this fascination with celebrity by running profiles of famous people. For example, television programs such as *Entertainment Tonight* devote all of their programming to stories about entertainment and entertainers. Magazines such as *People* fill their pages with stories of the private lives of famous people. Even newspapers, newsmagazines, and television news frequently delve into the lives of well-known personalities. Despite the number of articles and programs, few provide more than a superficial glimpse at their subjects.

Lucent's People in the News series offers young readers a deeper look into the lives of today's newsmakers, the influences that have shaped them, and the impact they have had in their fields of endeavor and on other people's lives. The subjects of the series hail from many disciplines and walks of life. They include authors, musicians, athletes, political leaders, entertainers, entrepreneurs, and others who have made a mark on modern life and who, in many cases, will continue to do so for years to come.

These biographies are more than factual chronicles. Each book emphasizes the contributions, accomplishments, or deeds that have brought fame or notoriety to the individual and shows how that person has influenced modern life. Authors portray their subjects in a realistic, unsentimental light. For example, Bill Gates—the cofounder and chief executive officer of the software giant Microsoft—has been instrumental in making personal computers the most vital tool of the modern age. Few dispute his business savvy, his perseverance, or his technical expertise, yet critics say he is ruthless in his dealings with competitors and driven more by his desire to maintain Microsoft's dominance in the computer industry than by an interest in furthering technology.

In these books, young readers will encounter inspiring stories about real people who achieved success despite enormous obstacles. Oprah Winfrey—the most powerful, most watched, and wealthiest woman on television today—spent the first six years of her life in the care of her grandparents while her unwed mother sought work and a better life elsewhere. Her adolescence was colored by promiscuity, pregnancy at age fourteen, rape, and sexual abuse.

Each author documents and supports his or her work with an array of primary and secondary source quotations taken from diaries, letters, speeches, and interviews. All quotes are footnoted to show readers exactly how and where biographers derive their information and provide guidance for further research. The quotations enliven the text by giving readers eyewitness views of the life and accomplishments of each person covered in the People in the News series.

In addition, each book in the series includes photographs, annotated bibliographies, timelines, and comprehensive indexes. For both the casual reader and the student researcher, the People in the News series offers insight into the lives of today's newsmakers—people who shape the way we live, work, and play in the modern age.

Fidel Castro: A Cold War Survivor

On January 8, 1959, Fidel Castro rode triumphantly into Havana, Cuba, on a tank. The powerful armed vehicle was a fitting symbol of the military might Castro had used in the Cuban Revolution to win control of the island nation from dictator Fulgencio Batista. The tank bearing Castro made its way through an even stronger weapon that had helped Castro achieve victory—the Cuban people who had supported him. As the tank rolled through Cuba's capital city, a crowd of more than one million people chanted "Fidel! Fidel! Fidel!" and many houses along the way bore signs that read "Fidel, esta es tu casa (Fidel, this is your house)."

Castro told his fellow Cubans he wanted to give them a better life than they had had under Batista. He also promised that he would only rule as long as they wanted him. "The day the people want, I shall leave,"[1] Castro said. No one could have predicted then that the bearded guerrilla fighter clad in green fatigues would remain in power for nearly a half-century. It was not until February 19, 2008, that the eighty-one-year-old Castro, weakened by age and illness, announced that he did not wish to be reappointed Cuba's president. In an article in the *Daily Granma*, Cuba's official newspaper, Castro wrote that it was finally time to let others govern Cuba:

My elemental duty is not to cling to positions, much less to stand in the way of younger persons, but rather to contribute my own experience and ideas whose modest value comes from the exceptional era that I had the privilege of living in.[2]

Five days later his brother, Raúl, was appointed his successor. Despite the change of leaders, most analysts speculated that Fidel would continue to be Cuba's *jefe máximo* (supreme leader) by continuing to influence decisions the Cuban government made. Thus, even his resignation as president was just another example of how the wily Castro had managed to hold on to power longer than any Communist leader the world has ever known.

Fidel Castro laughs at a 1959 newspaper headline announcing the discovery of a plot to assassinate him, one of many alleged attempts to oust the Cuban leader throughout his five decades in power.

The Last Cold War Leader

The armed revolution Castro led to victory came during the Cold War, the political, economic, and military battle between Communist and democratic nations that dominated the second half of the twentieth century. The Cold War began at the end of World War II when the Union of Soviet Socialist Republics (USSR) forced Eastern European nations like Poland and Hungary to become Communist. The United States and other democratic nations opposed communism's economic and political policies and began fighting to stop its spread to other countries. Despite their efforts, China, Korea, Vietnam, and Cuba all became Communist in the next two decades.

Cuba was the least powerful economically and politically of the Communist nations embroiled in that historic conflict; however, its proximity to the United States—Cuba lies less than 100 miles (161km) south of the straits of Florida—made it the flashpoint for the Cold War's deadliest episode. In October 1962, the Cuban Missile Crisis nearly caused a nuclear war between the United States and USSR. The crisis began when U.S. officials learned that the USSR, at Castro's invitation, had installed missiles in Cuba that could strike U.S. cities if launched. President John F. Kennedy ordered the USSR to remove the missiles. The Soviets refused, and for several tense days the two superpowers seemed to hover on the brink of nuclear war, which could have killed millions of people. The incident ended when the USSR finally backed down and removed the missiles.

The crisis made U.S. officials more determined than ever to get rid of Castro. Their first attempt to remove him from power had failed a year earlier, in April 1961, when U.S. intelligence officials helped Cuban exiles plan an invasion at the Bay of Pigs in Cuba. Castro, however, learned of the invasion, and Cuban soldiers defeated the exiles when they tried to land on the island. In the decades since the missile crisis, the United States has tried to isolate Cuba economically and to weaken Castro's regime politically enough to topple him. It is also believed that U.S. officials have unsuccessfully tried several times to assassinate Castro. But ten U.S. presidents have failed to oust Castro. Lorenzo Meyer, a professor of Latin American history at the College of Mexico, claims: "There is no other leader who was able to confront the United States for half a century and survive."[3]

Castro lived long enough to see the deaths of foes like U.S. presidents Kennedy and Ronald Reagan as well as more famous and powerful Communist leaders such as Soviet premier Nikita Khrushchev and the People's Republic of China's Mao Zedong. Castro, in fact, stayed in power even after the death of the Cold War itself. That historic conflict unofficially ended in the early 1990s when the nations that made up the USSR disbanded, and Communist nations such as China became more friendly with democratic nations.

How Castro Stayed in Power

Castro was able to retain control of Cuba because he used his power as a dictator to eliminate all political opposition. When Castro defeated Batista he killed or imprisoned thousands of government and army officials who opposed him. For five decades Castro's government has continued to punish, imprison, or kill anyone who criticized him or his government.

At nearly eighty years old, Castro addresses Cuban citizens in a live television broadcast in 2005. Critics attribute Castro's political longevity to his policy of oppression and brutality against those who oppose him.

Vladimiro Roca was one person brave enough to dare criticize Castro's regime. Roca was one of the first Cubans trained as a jet fighter pilot. He later worked for several decades as a Cuban government official. Roca began criticizing Castro in the 1990s because he realized Castro's political and economic policies had made life difficult for Cubans. In addition to being denied political and personal freedom, many Cubans were living in poverty because the nation's economy was weak. Roca was fired from his job for his comments.

In 1997, Roca and three other people published an attack of Castro's policies titled "The Homeland Belongs To Us." He was imprisoned for five years for his comments. When Castro announced he was stepping down as president, most Cubans were afraid to say anything negative about him because they feared punishment. Roca, however, dared to say that Castro had not been a good leader: "He's done some terrible things, but he's not crazy. A crazy man has no responsibility for his actions. And Fidel is responsible for everything that has happened in this country."[4]

A Great Nose for Danger

Roca has met Castro several times. Although there are many things about Castro he does not like, Roca admits that the Communist leader has one talent that has proved invaluable. "He was a very suspicious type and never trusted anyone," said Roca. "It has helped make him such a great survivor and political operator. He had a great nose for any danger or threat."[5]

Chapter 1

Growing Up Wealthy but Rebellious

The greatest irony in the life of Fidel Castro is that he was born into a rich family. Once Castro became a Communist, he considered capitalists his enemy. Capitalists are people who own land, factories, or other businesses and profit from the work done by people they hire. Castro's father, Angel Castro y Argiz, was a capitalist because he owned or leased 26,000 acres (10,522ha) of land and paid people to grow sugarcane. When Castro was born, his father even named him after one of his wealthy business friends, Fidel Piño. In a 1959 interview, Castro tried to explain why the son of a rich man grew up to be a Communist:

All the circumstances surrounding my life and childhood, everything I saw, would have made it logical to suppose I would develop the habits, the ideas, and the sentiments natural to a social class [capitalists] with certain privileges and selfish motives that make it indifferent to the problems of others. One circumstance helped [me] develop a certain human spirit: It was the fact that all our friends, our companions, were the sons of local peasants.[6]

Many of Castro's playmates, including children of people who worked for his father, were so poor that they did not own shoes and often did not have enough food to eat. Their poverty bothered Castro and made him start thinking at an early age that it was unjust for some people to be rich while others were poor.

Those feelings, however, did not stop Castro from enjoying the benefits of his family's wealth while he was growing up.

A Wealthy Landowner's Son

Fidel Alejandro Castro Ruz was born on August 13, 1926. Castro claims his father came to Cuba as a soldier to fight against the United States in the Spanish-American War in 1898, but there is no proof of that. Most historians believe Castro's father was a poor thirteen-year-old orphan in Spain who moved to Cuba in 1895 to live with an uncle. Castro's mother was Lina Ruz Gonzalez. Although Latin Americans honor their mothers by using their mothers' maiden name as a second last name, they are usually known in other countries only by their father's last name. Thus Fidel Castro is known to the world simply as Castro instead of Castro Ruz.

Fidel grew up on Finca Manacas (Palm Farm), his father's plantation in Birán in Oriente Province in eastern Cuba. Birán was a very small community that consisted of only a few homes, a small school, and several businesses. The Castro residence was the biggest home, but it was not elegant. His father built the house atop wooden pylons more than 6 feet (1.8m) tall so the family's cows, pigs, and geese could shelter and sleep beneath the

Castro was born in 1926 in this home on his family's plantation in Birán, a small community in eastern Cuba.

Growing Up Rich

No doubt what has had the greatest influence on me is that where I was born, I lived with people of the most humble origins. I remember the illiterate unemployed men who would stand in line near the cane fields, with nobody to bring them a drop of water, or breakfast, or lunch, or give them shelter, or transport. And I can't forget those children going barefoot. All the children whom I played with in Birán, all those I grew up with, ran around with, all over the place, were very, very poor. Some of them, at lunchtime, I would bring them a big can full of the food that was left over from meals at my house. I would go with them down to the river, on horseback or on foot, with my dogs, all over the place, to throw rocks, to hunt birds—a terrible thing but it was common to use a slingshot. On the other hand, in Santiago and later in Havana, I went to schools for the privileged; there were definitely landowners' children there.

Fidel Castro and Ignacio Ramonet, *Fidel Castro: My Life*. New York: Scribner, 2008, p. 42.

house. When Castro was young, the house was lit by candles and kerosene lamps because there was no electricity. Transportation was by horse or ox-cart over dirt roads that turned to mud when it rained. It was a primitive area, and most people were poor. Castro remembers that he and his siblings were treated differently because of their father's wealth: "We were considered rich and treated as such. I was brought up with all the privileges attendant to a son in such a family. Everyone lavished attention on me, flattered, and treated me differently from the other boys we played with when we were children."[7]

Life in the Castro home was very simple. When Castro's mother, Lina, wanted to call the family to eat, she would fire off a pistol. She was reportedly a poor housekeeper, and the home was cluttered and often dirty. The Castros also ate standing up, a habit Castro retained as an adult, and one that puzzled many people who later saw him eating that way. Fidel's father did not have much education, and his mother did not learn to read and write until she was an adult. But Fidel enjoyed learning, and his father's wealth allowed him to get a fine education.

Castro Goes to School

Castro first attended Birán's small school. He admits that he was not a very good student and that he disliked the teacher so much that he would sometimes swear at her and then run home. Castro, who had an explosive temper, said one such outburst resulted in his being injured:

> One day, I had just sworn at the teacher, and was racing down the rear corridor. I took a leap and landed on a board from a guava-jelly box with a nail in it. As I fell, the nail stuck in my tongue. When I got back home, my mother said to me: 'God punished you for swearing at the teacher.' I didn't have the slightest doubt that it was really true.[8]

When Fidel was six years old, his parents sent him and several siblings to live with and be educated by a teacher in Santiago de Cuba, a town on Cuba's southern coast that was the capital of Oriente Province. When that did not work out, his family enrolled the children in the first grade of the Colegio de La Salle, a Roman Catholic elementary school. Castro and his brothers Ramón and Raúl kept getting into trouble at school—Fidel, for example, fought with both students and priests—and after he finished the fourth grade his father said he would not let them return there. Castro pleaded with his mother to go back to the school despite the problems he was causing. "And that's when I did a terrible thing," Castro told one biographer. "I said that if they didn't send me to school I was going to burn the house down."[9]

Whether it was the young boy's threat of violence or his desire for education, his family let him return to school. This time, however, Castro's father enrolled his sons in the Colegio de Dolores, a

A teenaged Castro, second from right, is joined by other boys at Colegio de Dolores, a Jesuit school in Santiago, Cuba, in this 1940 photo.

Catholic school run by Jesuit priests. Jesuits are known for their tough discipline and high academic standards. At the school, Castro had to wear a tie, white pants, and dark blue jacket. His studies were harder than at his previous school, but Castro still found time for sports such as soccer, basketball, and baseball. Raúl Castro remembers that his brother flourished despite the discipline and the long hours of church and prayer that were also required: "He dominated the situation. He succeeded in everything. In sports, in studies. And, every day, he would fight. He had a very explosive character. He challenged the biggest and strongest ones, and when he was beaten, he started it all over again the next day. He would never quit."[10]

Fidel graduated from Dolores in 1941 when he was fourteen. That fall, he began attending the Colegio de Belén (Bethlehem), a Jesuit high school in Havana, Cuba's capital city. Belén was considered Cuba's elite high school, and its pupils included children from the island's richest and most powerful families. Castro once

Castro's 1945 yearbook photo was accompanied by a caption that predicted a "bright future" for the prospective law student.

again thrived academically even though teachers demanded a lot from their students. Although Castro himself is not religious, years later he credited the Jesuit priests with aiding his development as a leader. "The Jesuits clearly influenced me with their strict organization, their discipline and their values," he admitted.[11]

Castro graduated from Belén in 1945 and began attending law school at Havana University. He once said that when he was in his teens, his mother began telling him he should become a lawyer so that he could help protect the family's land and wealth against legal attacks. "At this period, our mother was full of advice," Castro said, explaining that she would tell him, "'Fidel, you must study and be diligent. And with all the talking you do, some day you will manage to become a lawyer!'"[12]

It was at Havana University that Castro started to form the political ideas that would lead to the Cuban Revolution.

Castro's Political Education

When Castro entered Havana University, he knew almost nothing about politics. But the school was a hotbed of political dissent, and he soon became involved in the heated discussions about his country's future. This is how Castro describes his political awakening at the school: "When I was 18, I was, politically speaking, illiterate [because] I didn't come from a family of politicians or grow up in a political atmosphere. I had the feeling that a new field was opening up for me. I started thinking about my country's political problems."[13]

Castro's growing interest in politics led him to read many books about political theory. He became convinced that capitalism was a bad system because it made too many people poor, like his childhood friends in Birán who had no shoes to wear. Although Castro would not call himself a Communist until many years later, he studied about communism and began to consider whether that philosophy suited him. Castro also began to believe that it was important for Cuba and other Latin American countries to become independent and to eliminate U.S. interference in their affairs.

Cuba in 1945 was governed by its president, Ramón Grau San Martín, who was unpopular. Castro opposed Grau because he was corrupt, ruled inefficiently, and had broken his 1944 campaign promise to distribute land to the poor. Castro was also angry that Grau allowed the United States government and American organized crime syndicates, which operated hotels and gambling casinos in Havana, to wield so much control over Cuba's economy. The United States had heavily influenced Cuba since it had freed it from Spain in 1898 in the Spanish-American War, and much of its influence was due to its being the largest purchaser of sugar, Cuba's economic mainstay.

Castro began criticizing Grau in speeches at rallies on campus and participating in demonstrations against him. Castro had always had a violent nature, and this personality trait served him well in Cuba's volatile style of politics. During this period in Cuba, opposing political groups often engaged each other in gang-style fights. Castro battled his political opponents with abandon in pitched street clashes. He once admitted of his violent student days that "I was the Don Quixote of the university, always under the guns and bullets."[14] Quixote is the hero of the novel by Miguel de Cervantes who tries to right injustice, and Castro saw himself playing the same political role then and in the future.

The violence between rival students groups included many murders. Castro was accused several times of killing political opponents, including Leonel Gomez, whom he allegedly shot to death in December 1946. Castro was never charged with murdering anyone; however, Rafael Díaz-Balart, one of Castro's closest friends at the University of Havana, claimed Castro did kill Gomez. Díaz-Balart, who was also from Oriente Province, was a member of a prominent political family. The two young Cubans were drawn together by their love of politics, and both dreamed of one day becoming president of Cuba. They would become political enemies as adults because Díaz-Balart supported Batista. Díaz-Balart left Cuba for the United States when Castro succeeded in winning control of their country because he believed Castro was a Communist. On May 3, 1969, in an appearance before a U.S. Senate committee, Díaz-Balart testified that Castro shot Gomez. When Díaz-Balart was asked how he knew, he answered, "Because Fidel Castro told me. He invited me to participate with him in the killing of that student and I refused because I am a Christian."[15]

The deep-seated political beliefs that Castro developed and his urge to do something about them led him into his first two attempts at creating revolution. Both were in other countries, and both were failures.

Fidel Castro Writes a Letter to a U.S. President

On November 6, 1940, thirteen-year-old Fidel Castro wrote to U.S. president Franklin D. Roosevelt. The letter was on stationery from the Colegio de Delores in Santiago, the school Castro attended. Although there are grammar mistakes, Castro was able to communicate well in English for someone whose native language was Spanish. In the letter, which today is part of the U.S. National Archives, Castro wrote:

> My good friend Roosevelt: I don't know very [good] English, but I know as much as write to you. I like to hear the radio, and I am very happy, because I heard in it, that you will be president of a new era. [If] you like, give me a ten dollars bill green american, in the letter, because never, I have not seen a ten dollars bill green american and I would like to have one of them. Thank you very much. Good by. Your friend, Fidel Castro.

President Roosevelt responded to Castro, who posted the letter on a school bulletin board. However, the president did not send the future revolutionary a ten-dollar bill.

A letter from Fidel Castro to President Franklin D. Roosevelt. National Archives and Records Administration. http://www.archives.gov/exhibits/american_originals/castro.html.

Young Castro's 1940 letter to President Franklin D. Roosevelt is housed at the U.S. National Archives.

The Traveling Revolutionary

In July 1947, Castro joined a group of twelve hundred men from several Latin American countries who wanted to overthrow dictator Rafael Trujillo, who had ruled the Dominican Republic for nearly two decades. Trujillo was in power because the United States backed his corrupt regime, which brutally repressed any opposition. Castro still had several final examinations to pass in his third year of law school, but he believed it was more important to attack a brutal dictator. "I considered that my first duty was to enroll as a soldier in the expedition and I did so,"[16] he said. Castro trained for the invasion for fifty-nine days on Cayo Confites, a small island in a remote part of Cuba.

President Grau, however, learned about the planned invasion and on September 20 ordered the force to disband. Even though some people involved in the attempt quit, Castro and others decided to go ahead with the plan. They departed Cuba on September 28 on the ship Fantasma, but the Cuban navy intercepted the vessel shortly after departure. To avoid capture, Castro and some others jumped into the Bay of Nipe, which is infested with sharks, and swam almost 9 miles (14.5km) to shore.

Castro made his way home to Birán and then returned to school. The incident made him interested in political efforts by students in other Latin American countries. In April 1948, Castro helped organize the Pan-American Union Conference, a gathering of students from Latin American countries. They met in Bogotá, the capital of Colombia, a country that was in the midst of a civil war.

Violence flared in Bogotá on April 9, after liberal leader Jorge Eliécer Gaitán was shot to death. His assassination ignited a series of riots and pitched battles that claimed the lives of more than thirty-five hundred people and is known today as El Bogotázo, the violence in Bogotá. Castro had met with Gaitán two days earlier, and the politically motivated assassination inflamed him. "I joined the people. I witnessed the spectacle of a totally spontaneous popular revolution,"[17] Castro said. He and the other Cubans watched the street battles between political parties bent on winning control of Colombia. Castro even delivered a speech to rally people to overthrow the current government.

The students eventually sought refuge in the Cuban embassy, and on April 13, Cuban officials flew them home. Colombian officials charged that Cuban Communists had helped incite the violence. Castro has denied the claim, saying, "As young, idealistic, Don Quixote-like students, we simply joined in the people's rebellion."[18] Castro also claims he was not a Communist in this period even though he had studied Communist political and economic theories. Back in Cuba again, Castro returned to his law studies at Havana University.

Lawyer and Husband

Castro continued to be involved in Cuban politics through activities on campus and by writing articles for one of Havana's fourteen newspapers. He continued his law school studies and even found time to romance Mirta Díaz-Balart, his friend Rafael's sister, who was also a Havana University student. Castro had met her two years earlier through her brother. Mirta was beautiful and from one of Cuba's richest families; her father was mayor of Banes in Oriente Province, a community not far from where Castro was born. Castro was not very romantic—unlike most Cubans he did not like to dance, and he never gave her flowers—but the couple fell in love.

Castro's son Fidelito, left, was born in 1949, the first of seven children fathered by the Cuban leader.

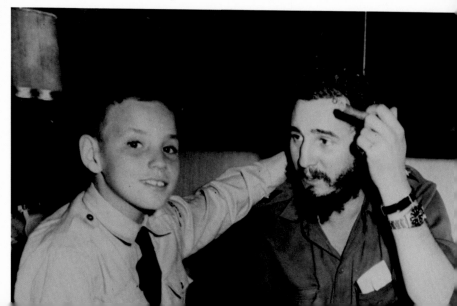

Castro and Mirta were married on October 12, 1948, in a Roman Catholic church in Banes. When Mirta's father gave them ten thousand dollars for a honeymoon, the couple decided to visit the United States. They began their trip in Miami and in December went to New York. The newlyweds lived and dined lavishly in the best hotels on their honeymoon. Castro, who later as Cuba's Communist leader would come to condemn such excesses, delighted in the privileged life he led. "I am not going to deny that I enjoyed some of Miami's magnificent comforts. For the first time, I knew a T-bone steak, smoked salmon, and those things that I, a youth with a big appetite, appreciated a lot."[19]

In New York Castro reportedly bought a copy of *Das Kapital*, the book by Karl Marx that provided the basic philosophy for communism. But he also purchased a white Lincoln Continental car that he had shipped back to Cuba. When the Castros returned to Cuba, they lived in an apartment in Havana while Castro went back to law school. On September 1, 1949, their first child was born. The couple followed Cuban tradition by naming their son after his father. His full name was Fidel Castro Díaz-Balart but they called him Fidelito, which means "little Fidel."

Castro graduated from Havana University in September 1950 with a Doctor of Law degree. He said he was able to pass his tests despite missing so many classes because of his excellent memory; he had the ability to study hard for final exams and retain enough knowledge to pass them. His almost photographic memory was a mental tool that helped him greatly all his life.

Consumed by Politics

It was that ability to learn a lot in short, intensive bursts of study that enabled Castro to neglect his classes much of the time so that he could participate in his true love, political action. Herminio Portela Vila was his professor for a course on Latin American history. A comment Vila made sums up why Castro was often an indifferent student even though he was very smart: "I had to flunk him. He was never there. Did he show interest in Hispanic America? He tried to make [history], not study it."[20]

Chapter 2

Castro's Failed Revolution

One of the wedding guests who attended the marriage of Fidel and Mirta Castro on October 12, 1948, was Fulgencio Batista, a former president of Cuba. Batista was a friend of both families, and he gave the happy couple a pair of five-hundred-dollar bills to spend on their honeymoon in the United States. On that same day, Carlos Prío Socarrás was inaugurated president of Cuba. In the next few years the lives of Castro, Batista, and Prío would become intertwined in a series of dramatic events as the trio battled for political control of their island home.

The most daring and foolhardy attempt to seize power would come from Castro, the youngest and least politically powerful of the three men. Castro had once written in the margins of a book he was reading, "I prefer to die riddled with bullets than to live humiliated."[21] Castro, however, would live to be humiliated after his bungled attempt to oust Batista through military force. But the disgrace from his failure would only set the stage for the Cuban Revolution, whose slogan would be "Patria o Muerte!" (Fatherland or Death!).

The Political Candidate

Castro in 1950 opened a law firm in Havana with two law school classmates—Jorge Aspiazo Nuñez de Villavicencio and Rafael Resende Viges. Castro, however, was more concerned about helping poor people to build a base for his future in politics than in

Fulgencio Batista celebrates his return to power in Cuba after a March 1952 military coup over President Carlos Prío.

being a successful lawyer. He actually made so little money that his father had to send him a monthly allowance so he and his family could survive.

The law firm's first job was to collect overdue bills from carpenters who had bought supplies from a lumber company. But when one carpenter came to pay his bill, Fidel told him "No, you need this money now, and our client does not."[22] The lawyers collected so little money that the lumber company fired them. Castro's law firm also specialized in cases in which the government had wronged average citizens. After a worker was killed by police during a riot on February 18, 1951, Castro tried to get officials to charge the policemen with murder. His effort failed, but it won Castro the admiration of many poor people who believed he was standing up for their interests against the government.

Castro also wrote articles for newspapers and gave speeches on radio attacking President Prío, who he claimed was corrupt and was hurting Cubans with his policies. He investigated Prío and on January 28, 1952, presented a list of charges against the president in the court of accounts, a national court. He claimed Prío was guilty of accepting bribes so that a child molester would stay out of prison, violating labor laws to take advantage of thousands of workers, and hurting the economy by selling farm products to other countries at prices below their true value. In a move that was calculated to make himself look like a patriot, Castro released the charges on the anniversary of the birth of Cuban hero José Martí.

The claims Castro made were true. They angered many people and helped Castro become more popular. He used his new fame in 1952 to run for a seat in the Cuban parliament as a representante (congressman) for the Partido Ortodoxo (Orthodox Party). His campaign for public office was the first step in his plan to rule Cuba. Castro wanted to be elected a legislator as part of his long-range plan of gaining political power so he could change Cuba's form of government:

> I conceived a strategy for the revolutionary seizure of power. Once in the Parliament, I would break party discipline and present [my own] program. I hoped, by proposing a program that recognized the most deeply felt aspirations of the majority of the population, to mobilize the great masses of farmers, workers, unemployed, teachers [and] intellectual workers.[23]

His vision for the future was reflected in his campaign promises. Castro wanted to end government corruption, make the government more responsive to the needs of poor people, and limit the control the U.S. government and U.S. business had over Cuban affairs. Castro's campaign was so successful that he was expected to win the election on June 1, but on March 10, Batista seized power from Prío through a military coup d'etat. The new Cuban dictator soon canceled the elections, a move that shattered Castro's dream of future power. Castro decided to fight back, first legally and then with a military coup of his own.

How Castro Won Converts

❝ Fidel could convince any person to do anything," Carlos Bustillo, who would be in the car behind Fidel at Moncada, remembered. And another [Moncada veteran], Gerardo Pérez Puelles, recalled that "Fidel had this way of captivating people. Maybe it is the warmness of his speech. He could get together with ten guys and he would have ten more recruits. He was very, very good at this." But his methods of winning people over depended as much on his example as his evocative words. One afternoon during weapons training on a farm, a rifle had been damaged. Fidel immediately began to look for a small spring that had fallen from it into the high grass. Everyone else soon gave up, but Fidel persisted, searching in the rain until he finally found the lost part. He turned then to his weary men and said triumphantly, "See, this shows that perseverance will bring about victory." That afternoon could have stood as a metaphor for his whole life.

Georgie Anne Geyer, *Guerrilla Prince: The Untold Story of Fidel Castro*. Boston: Little Brown and Company, 1991, p. 107.

Castro Challenges Batista

Ruben Fulgencio Batista Zaldívar took command of the Cuban army in a nearly bloodless seizure of power that met with nearly no resistance; only two men who tried to stop him died. The April 9, 1953, cover of *Time* magazine featured a photograph of Batista with a Cuban flag behind him and the caption "Cuba's Batista: he got past Democracy's sentries."[24]

It was actually the second time Batista had trampled democracy to win control of Cuba. On September 4, 1933, he had led other army leaders in a military coup known as the "Revolt of the Sergeants" to overthrow the government of President Carlos Manuel de Céspedes y Quesada. As chief of staff of the Cuban army in 1933, Batista had controlled military power, and he used it to gain political power as well. Even though the military takeover had been illegal, U.S. officials in 1933 recognized Batista as Cuba's leader because they felt he would stabilize Cuba.

In 1940, Batista was elected president of Cuba in the first elections held under a new constitution. When Batista was unable to run again in 1944 because of term limits, he moved to the United States and lived for four years in Daytona Beach, Florida. He then returned to Cuba in 1948 and was elected to the Cuban senate. He ran for president again in 1952, but when it became apparent that he would lose he decided to seize power. Friends of his in the army allowed him to take control of the government because they knew they would benefit from his rule.

U.S. president Dwight D. Eisenhower on March 27, 1952, formally recognized Batista's government. The United States welcomed back Batista because he was anti-Communist—the Cold War had already begun, and the United States almost blindly supported anyone who opposed communism—and friendly to U.S. business interests. Eisenhower acknowledged the new government even though Batista had scrapped Cuba's 1940 constitution, which guaranteed citizens basic rights that other democratic nations had. Batista did not want anyone to be able to challenge him as Cuba's ruler. In addition to destroying democracy, Batista was corrupt. He made government business deals that helped him and his friends profit at the expense of Cuban citizens. Batista also used government funds to help U.S. organized crime leaders such as Meyer Lansky and Lucky Luciano build lavish hotels and gambling casinos in Havana, which soon became known as the Latin Las Vegas.

On March 24, 1952, Castro filed a brief with the constitutional court in Havana that accused Batista of violating the Cuban constitution by using force to seize power. "Instead of progress and order," the brief said, "there is barbarism and brute force. [Batista's] crimes have incurred punishing deserving more than one hundred years of imprisonment."[25] Castro knew the brief would be ignored, because Batista controlled the courts too. He filed it mainly to justify his own attempt to take control of Cuba through military force, one that he was already planning.

The Power of the People

In his court speech on October 16, 1953, Fidel Castro proclaimed that the Cuban people could overcome Fulgencio Batista:

> [Batista] tried to establish the myth that modern arms render the people helpless to overthrow tyrants. Military parades and the pompous display of the machines of war are used to perpetuate this myth and to create in the people a complex of absolute impotence. But no weapon, no violence, can vanquish the people once they have decided to win back their rights. Both past and present are full of examples. Most recently there has been a revolt in Bolivia, where miners with dynamite sticks laid low the Regular Army regiments. But, fortunately, we Cubans need not look for examples abroad. No example is as inspiring as that of our own land. During the war of 1895, there were nearly half a million armed Spanish soldiers in Cuba, many more than the Dictator counts upon today to hold back a population five times greater. This is how the people fight when they want to win their liberty; they throw stones at airplanes and overturn tanks!

Fidel Castro, "History Will Absolve Me." Excerpts from his own defense, delivered at his trial, October 16, 1953. http://social.chass.ncsu.edu/slatta/hi216/documents/dabsolve.html.

Fidel Plots His Own Takeover

Castro went into hiding when Batista seized power because he feared the dictator would arrest people such as himself who could challenge him politically. On March 16, Castro met with fellow Ortodoxo members in Colón cemetery, where they had gathered to honor a former party leader. Castro told them, "If Batista grabbed power by force, he must be thrown out by force!"[26] He continued to make similar threats against the Batista regime in newspaper articles and speeches to small groups as he attempted to rally the public to rise up against Batista.

In the next few months Castro traveled thousands of miles and met with hundreds of people to recruit a private army for his attempt to seize power from Batista. He had to operate in secret to avoid arrest. Castro refused to align himself with Cuban Communists because he wanted to lead the fight against Batista himself. Years later, Castro admitted that he won people to his cause more quickly than he could have imagined: "It went relatively quickly. I was amazed at how fast, using the right arguments and a number of examples, you could persuade somebody that the society [we lived in] was absurd and had to be changed."[27] One of his converts was Melba Hernández, a lawyer who later admitted she joined Castro because the force of his personality and arguments overwhelmed her: "I think this happened to everybody: From the moment you shake hands with Fidel, you are impressed."[28]

Castro claimed he recruited twelve hundred followers during this period. He also raised thousands of dollars to buy guns, rifles, and grenades for them. Castro even asked his father for $3,000. Angel Castro, however, thought his son was crazy to challenge Batista. "It's really stupid," he told Fidel, "to think that you and that group of starving ragamuffins could bring down Batista, with all his tanks, cannons, and airplanes. Have a good trip, you loco [crazy person]. I hope nothing bad happens to you."[29] Despite his belief that his son would fail, Angel gave him $140.

Most of Castro's recruits were poor, uneducated, and had no military experience. The first time many of them fired a gun was in training sessions at Havana University, which had a firing range for students to use. Jesús Montané explained how easy it was for the rebels to use the firing range: "Everybody took part in rifle practice. I would say more than a thousand young people practiced in the university, at one time or another. We had made special arrangements and when we were practicing nobody else could."[30]

In February 1953, Castro began to consider where to strike Batista. He decided on the Moncada Barracks in Santiago de Cuba where he had gone to school as a child. Castro thought that if he was successful in capturing Moncada, thousands of Cubans would join his rebellion against Batista and he could arm them with weapons stored there. He set the attack for July 26.

The Attack on Moncada

Castro rented a small farm in the seaside town of Siboney that became a staging area for the attack and a place to store the weapons his group had acquired—light hunting rifles, shotguns, and a few U.S. military arms, including a Thompson submachine gun. Despite his claims to have many more men, Castro selected only 160 men and two women—Hernández and Haydee Santamaría—to participate in the attack. They met at the farm the night before the assault. Many had not known what the mission was, and ten refused to go when they found out, because they believed it was suicidal to attack a facility guarded by heavily armed soldiers.

At 3 A.M. on July 26, Castro gave the remaining rebels their final instructions and tried to calm their fears. "In a few hours,"

Castro, center, stands with fellow rebels in the days leading up to their attack on the Moncada Barracks in July 1953.

Castro said, "you will be victorious or defeated, but regardless of the outcome—listen well, compañéros (companions)!—this movement will triumph."[31] They left the farm at 5:15 A.M. in twenty-six cars to win control of Cuba.

The group was split into four parties. Castro led a group of ninety-five men in the main assault on Moncada while his brother Raúl and seven men went to secure the nearby Palace of Justice. The two women were among twenty-one rebels who tried to commandeer a civilian hospital, where they would care for anyone who was wounded. A second unit of twenty-seven men was dispatched to the Bayamó Barracks, which was 80 miles (128.75km) away, to stop them from coming to the aid of the Moncada soldiers once the attack began.

Castro had believed that homemade army uniforms would disguise his men so they could get past the guards. The scheme worked initially; several rebels got inside the complex, entered a dormitory, and held some sleepy soldiers at gunpoint. But a roving patrol spotted other rebels getting out of their civilian cars, and the two sides began fighting. The poorly armed rebels managed to kill nineteen soldiers and wound twenty-seven more before the army's superior numbers overwhelmed them, forcing Castro and the others to flee for their lives. Castro said it did not take him long to realize the attempt was going to fail: "I believed that no more than thirty minutes had passed, maybe much less, when I resigned myself to the fact that the objective was now impossible. I knew the details better than anyone, and I knew on what basis that decision [to retreat] had to be made."[32]

Only eight of Castro's men died during the fighting, but the soldiers murdered sixty-one of the rebels after taking them prisoner. They also brutally tortured the men to get information. Santamaría later revealed how brutal the soldiers had been toward the rebels. While being held prisoner, she was approached by a soldier carrying an eyeball, who told her, "This belongs to your brother, and if you don't tell us what he refused to tell us, we'll gouge his other one out too."[33] Though she loved her brother, she refused to answer their questions. The order to torture and kill the rebels had come from Batista, and only the two women and a few male rebels survived.

Cuban government soldiers take action to defend the Moncada Barracks after the rebel attack in July 1953.

Castro claimed his plan failed because the patrol accidentally spotted his men and because the most heavily armed part of his force was delayed in getting to the scene of the fight. "Our reserve division, which had almost all our heavy weapons, made a wrong turn and completely lost its way in a city that was unfamiliar to them,"[34] Castro said. Historians, however, believe Castro did not have enough men and weapons to seize the barracks even if everything had gone as planned. Historians also doubt whether the public would have risen up against Batista as Castro had hoped, for he would have needed their support for his revolt to succeed.

"History Will Absolve Me"

About half the rebels, including Castro and his brother, escaped when the attack failed. Castro sought sanctuary by hiding in the rugged Sierra Maestra, a nearby mountain range, with several other men, but on the morning of August 1 they were captured while sleeping in an abandoned hut by a sixteen-man army patrol led by Lieutenant Pedro Manuel Sarría Tartabull. One of the soldiers called Castro an assassin for killing soldiers at Moncada. Castro, even though he was ringed by soldiers with rifles pointing at him, responded angrily, "It is you who are assassins.... It is you who kill unarmed prisoners.... You are the soldiers of a tyrant!" When some soldiers told Sarría they wanted to kill Castro and his fellow rebels, he shouted at them, "No, don't kill them! I order you not to kill them! I am in command here. You can't kill ideas. You can't kill ideas!"[35]

Castro was among twenty-nine rebels captured after the failed mission. He was tried on September 21 for violating the Social Defense Code by trying to overthrow the government. Castro acted as his own lawyer in the trial, which lasted until October 16, 1953, and on its final day he delivered his most famous speech. The speech—titled "La Historia me absolvera" (History Will Absolve Me)—was a denunciation of Batista and a political statement of how Castro would govern Cuba. Castro said he would bring back the 1940 constitution Batista had scrapped, give land to poor farmers, allow workers to share profits with their employers, and end government corruption. It was a bittersweet declaration of what Castro wanted to do because he knew he was going to prison. He ended the speech by saying: "As for me, I know that imprisonment will be harder for me than it ever has been for anybody, filled with cowardly threats and hideous cruelty. But I do not fear it, as I do not fear the fury of the wretched tyrant who snuffed out the lives of seventy [rebel] brothers of mine. Condemn me. It does not matter. History will absolve me."[36]

Castro's speech was so powerful and dramatic that many people in the courtroom, even those who disagreed with what he was saying, were stunned into silence. Realizing the effect he had created, Castro pounded on a table and told everyone he was finished. His brave words did not sway the judge, who sentenced Castro to fifteen years in prison. Raúl and four others got prison terms of thirteen years. The rest of the rebels got shorter sentences, including only seven months for the women.

A New Beginning

Although Castro's revolution appeared to have ended as quickly as it had started, he began gaining new supporters even while he was in prison. The trial had been held in secret, but Castro's speech was smuggled out of prison and printed so thousands of people could read it. The bravery Castro showed in defying

Castro, center, answers questions posed by Cuban government officials after his arrest for leading rebel forces in the attack on the Moncada Barracks.

The Power of "La Historia me absolvera (history will absolve me)"

Marta Rojas, a journalist who heard Castro deliver his famous speech recalls:

> I was simply carried away by his words. The same was true with the [courtroom] guards. I was watching the guards standing with their weapons loose listening, carried away by Fidel. They were simply absorbed and engrossed by his words. When Fidel was through with his speech, there was silence.

Quoted in Peter G. Bourne, *Fidel*. New York: Dodd, Mead, 1986, p. 93.

the court and his promise to help the poor became the Cuban Revolution's most famous and effective piece of propaganda.

Santamaría said years later that the initial failure only made the rebels more determined to succeed. "It was at Moncada," she said, "that we were forged, where we got used to the sight of blood, to men suffering. To the struggle."[37]

Chapter 3

Castro Invades Cuba

When Fidel Castro proclaimed "La historia me absolvera! (History will absolve me!)"[38] during his trial for trying to overthrow dictator Fulgencio Batista, he was parroting a phrase another historical figure had used three decades earlier in an identical situation. Adolf Hitler first uttered that famous declaration in 1924 when he was tried after his unsuccessful attempt to seize power in Germany. While growing up during World War II, Castro admired both Hitler and Italian dictator Benito Mussolini for the way they ruthlessly wielded power to govern their countries and for their dramatic speaking styles. Marcelino Efal, a prominent Cuban psychiatrist, claims that Castro studied and adopted many of the traits of such leaders: "All the dictators have the same style, and Fidel was often studying the behavior and style of all of them: Mussolini, Hitler, [Vladimir] Lenin, [Joseph] Stalin, [Argentina's Juan] Peron. Everybody who could give him a feature to imitate and take advantage of."[39]

While attending Havana University, Castro imitated Mussolini's flamboyant speaking style while standing before a mirror and reciting into a recording device. He also read a Spanish edition of Hitler's famous book *Mein Kampf* (My Struggle; in Spanish, *La Lucha*). Hitler wrote *Mein Kampf* while he was in prison after being found guilty of treason. The book details Hitler's views about German racial superiority and the idea that a dictator who has complete control is the best leader for a nation. Castro rejected Hitler's racism but concurred with his belief about strong leaders.

Although Hitler in 1924 was sentenced to five years in prison, German officials released him nine months later because they did not believe he was powerful enough to take over Germany. But Hitler had continued to recruit supporters while he was in prison, and it took him only nine years after he was freed to become Germany's leader. Castro followed a similar path to become Cuba's leader, only he would succeed in half the time it took Hitler.

Prisoner No. 3859

Castro, his brother Raúl, and other rebels found guilty of trying to seize the Moncada Barracks were imprisoned on Isla de Piños (Isle of Pines), which lay 50 miles (80km) off Cuba's coast. Castro was now National Men's Reformatory Prisoner 3859. Like Hitler, Castro used his time in prison to refine his political ideas and plan for the future. In a letter he wrote, Castro claimed, "What a terrific school this prison is! Here I can shape my view of the world and perfect the meaning of my life."[40] Castro read and studied scores of books, from novels like Victor Hugo's Les Misérables, a tale about how the rich oppress the poor, to political works like Das Kapital, the book by Karl Marx that set down Communist economic and political principles.

In addition to studying, Castro lectured other prisoners on subjects like Cuban history, arithmetic, and geography and discussed political theories. His goal in teaching prisoners was to win future allies in his drive to become Cuba's leader. Castro also worked to woo new supporters on the outside through his trial speech. After the speech was smuggled out of prison, Castro ordered Melba Hernández to print and distribute 100,000 copies of it. "Our propaganda," Castro wrote, "must not let up for one minute, because it is the heart of the struggle."[41] There was only enough money, however, to print 27,500 copies. Castro thought the document was important because he considered it his version of Mein Kampf, which had won Hitler so much support.

Mug shots of Castro, left, his brother Raúl, center, and other rebel soldiers arrested after their attempt to take over the Moncada Barracks hang in a museum created at the farmhouse where Castro planned the attack.

While Castro was imprisoned, his wife, Mirta, struggled to support herself and their son, Fidelito. She received help from Fidel's family, and her brother, Rafael Díaz-Balart, who was an official in the Cuban government, got her a job with the Cuban Interior Ministry. Mirta visited Fidel often while he was in prison. But in July 1954, she filed for divorce. She did that after she discovered Castro had been having an affair with Natalia Revuelta, a woman from a rich Cuban family. Castro had been writing letters to both women. When he wrote to them both on the same day, the letters accidentally got mixed up and sent to the wrong women. After the divorce, she moved to the United States with Fidelito.

Castro had been sentenced to fifteen years in prison, but on May 7, 1955, Batista granted amnesty to him and other political prisoners. Batista had been elected president of Cuba, and he no longer felt Castro could harm him. On May 15, Castro left the Isle of Pines a free man after spending twenty-two months in prison.

The 26th of July Movement

In underestimating the threat Castro posed to him, Batista made the same mistake German officials had made forty-one years earlier when they released Hitler because they did not think he was capable of gaining power. But while Castro was in prison, he had begun creating a network of supporters to help him overthrow Batista. He named this group the 26th of July Movement—it's abbreviated nickname was M-26-7—after the date of his attack on Moncada Barracks. Castro has always claimed the Cuban Revolution started that day even though the attack was a failure.

A Dedicated Revolutionary

One reason Fidel Castro was able to win allies for his planned invasion of Cuba was that he was so dedicated to his cause. Orlando de Cardenás, a Cuban whom Castro met in Mexico City, helped him obtain weapons. De Cardenás said that Castro impressed him with his devotion to winning control of Cuba:

> What struck me was the way he concentrated one hundred percent absolutely on his goals. There were no women, no play. Many times I told my wife, "Fidel is not a Cuban at all, he doesn't like music, he doesn't drink." His only vice was smoking Cuban cigars. From time to time a box would arrive from Cuba. He would distribute the cigars among the others and keep one or two for himself. No hot or cold weather would affect him. He would work eighteen, twenty hours a day. Many times I asked myself, "When does he sleep?" He was always interviewing people so they would help him.

Peter G. Bourne, *Fidel*. New York: Dodd, Mead, 1986, p. 120.

Castro's new attempt to oust Batista began on the boat ride back to the Cuban mainland from his island prison. He wrote an article that was a declaration of political war against Batista. Printed in the newspaper *La Calle*, Castro's article announced, "As we leave the prison we proclaim that we shall struggle for [our] ideas even at the price of our existence. Our freedom shall not be feast or rest, but battle and duty for a nation without despotism or misery.... Despots vanish, peoples remain."[42]

Castro's stay in Cuba was brief. He quickly earned Batista's wrath with speeches he made and articles he wrote criticizing the way Batista ruled Cuba. Castro soon began to fear that the dictator would use violence to silence him. Castro also knew that it would be impossible to create an armed revolt while he was in Cuba because Batista's spy network would discover his plans and eliminate him and his supporters. Castro decided to go to Mexico, where he would be safe to work out his plan to topple Batista.

Before Castro left, he sent a letter to major political leaders that explained he was not giving up his fight against Batista: "As a follower of Martí, I believe the hour has come to take our rights and not beg for them, to fight instead of pleading for them."[43] And like Martí, Castro had already decided on how he would defeat Batista—he would invade Cuba as his political hero had done in 1895 to free its people from Spanish rule.

Castro departed Cuba on July 7, 1955. The next time Castro set foot on Cuban soil, it would be as the leader of an armed force of invaders.

Castro Plans an Invasion

Cubans had been fleeing their homeland for decades to escape brutal, repressive rulers like Batista. Many of them went to Mexico City, a large city that was an amiable home for Spanish-speaking people. Castro began enlisting Cubans already living in Mexico City to provide financial backing and other help in staging his invasion. Castro's charismatic personality helped him win converts to his cause such as Orlando de Cardenás, a former associate of deposed Cuban president Carlos Prío. De Cardenás said of

Castro delivers a passionate address to expatriate Cubans during his visit to New York City in October 1955 in order to drum up money and support for a rebel invasion that would oust Batista's government.

Castro, "He had a power of convincing that was tremendous."[44] The Cuban exile agreed to help Castro get weapons for the invasion.

Several men who helped Castro storm the Moncada Barracks volunteered for the invasion, but he also recruited other participants. One was a young doctor from Argentina named Ernesto Guevara de La Serna, who would become world famous by a nickname his Cuban companions gave him—"Che," an Argentine slang word for "buddy." Raúl met Guevara first and introduced him to his brother in August 1955. The two men liked each other immediately and talked for hours. Both of them believed capitalism was hurting average people, wanted to give land to poor farmers, and felt the United States wielded too much economic and political power in Latin America. "I talked with Fidel throughout the night," Guevara said. "By morning I was already enlisted as a doctor in the forthcoming expedition [invasion]."[45]

To make sure Cubans did not forget him, Castro wrote several political documents after he arrived in Mexico City. In "Manifesto Number One of the 26 of July Movement to the People of Cuba," Castro criticized Batista and promised to overthrow him. Castro had copies of it printed and shipped to Cuba so his followers could distribute them. Castro was so broke, however, that he had to pawn his overcoat to pay for them.

In October, Castro went on a fund-raising trip to U.S. cities like New York, Philadelphia, Tampa, and Miami to seek money from expatriate Cubans like Prío. In a speech in New York, Castro

A Botched Invasion

Fidel Castro talks about the 1956 invasion:

We landed on December 2, 1956, with 82 men, and had our first setback. After a week at sea in a tiny boat, battered by storms, and with our supplies almost gone, [we] landed, hungry and weak. First, we had the bad luck to come ashore in a terrible place, a real swamp, we took a beating, wading through mud for several hours to reach solid ground. Then, after three days without food, marching through strange country without a guide, we were surprised and routed by land forces far superior in number and by an aircraft squadron. Only a few of our men were killed, but our group was completely dispersed. I had two men and two rifles with me; and eight men and seven rifles were with my brother Raúl. When we two managed to regroup, we had twelve men and eleven rifles. All the other weapons were lost or hidden. Several of our comrades, who had hidden their guns in places they couldn't remember at all, got together with us again. Others were captured by the army and killed.

Quoted in Carlos Franqui, *Diary of the Cuban Revolution*. New York: Viking, 1980, p. 129.

brashly told an audience that "I can inform you with complete certainty that in 1956, we [he and his men] will be free or we will be martyrs."[46] Castro meant that by then he and his men would either have ousted Batista or they would have died trying. He returned to Mexico City on December 10 and began training his men for the invasion.

The Guerilleros Train

Castro and the men he chose to invade Cuba considered themselves *guerrilleros*, the Spanish word for guerrilla, a soldier who fights in an irregular manner. They trained on a ranch near Mexico City under Alberto Bayo, a Cuban who had been a general in the Spanish army and sympathized with Castro's plans to topple Batista. Bayo taught the rebels how to handle weapons, survive in the wilderness, march long distances at night, and climb mountains. They were skills Castro's men would need in fighting Batista from Cuba's jungles and mountains, where they would take refuge from Batista's soldiers between attacks.

Castro and his men toughened their bodies in Mexico City's Chapultepec Park where they rowed boats and climbed trees. Popocatépetl, a dormant volcano near Mexico City, became Guevara's personal training ground. Guevara suffered from asthma, but he was determined to climb the 18,000-foot (5,000m) mountain to prove he could do something that hard. Guevara never succeeded, but Castro said his repeated attempts showed his fierce determination: "He never made it to the top, he never reached the top of Popocatépetl. But he kept trying to climb the mountain, and he'd have spent his entire life trying to climb Popocatépetl. That gives you some idea of his spiritual strength, his constancy."[47]

Despite Castro's efforts to keep the preparations secret, Cuban spies learned that he was planning some type of action against Batista. The Cuban dictator contacted Mexican officials and on June 25, 1956, they arrested Castro and his men on an accusation that he was plotting to overthrow Batista. Although some of his men were imprisoned until August, Castro was released on July 24 because officials did not have enough facts to charge him with a crime. When Castro was freed, however, he did not forget about his followers who were still in jail. He visited them and got them out as fast as he could. Guevara said the loyalty and concern that Castro always showed toward his men was one of the qualities that made his followers so devoted to him: "These personal attitudes that Fidel has with people whom he appreciates are the key to the fanaticism that he creates around him [and] to an adhesion to principle is added a personal adhesion, making this Rebel Army an indivisible block."[48] Castro's second stint in jail did little to derail his invasion plan. Once his men were all freed, he was able to go ahead with his grand scheme to seize power in Cuba.

Castro Invades Cuba

In October, Castro illegally entered the United States from Mexico by swimming across the Rio Grande to McAllen, Texas, to meet with Prío. The former Cuban president said he would give Castro one hundred thousand dollars for the invasion. Castro badly needed the money. His most important purchase with the funds he got from Prío was the *Granma* (Grandmother), a decrepit 38-foot (11.6m) boat that would ferry Castro and his men to Cuba.

On November 25, Castro and eighty-one men left the Mexican port city of Tuxpán for Cuba. Castro had wanted to bring fifty more men. It was impossible, however, because the small ship was already so heavily loaded with men and supplies that they feared it would capsize if more was put aboard. The journey of 1,150 miles (1,609km) took seven days, instead of the five Castro had expected, due to stormy weather; the waves were so large that everyone aboard became seasick. The ship ran aground on December 2, 60 yards (58m) off shore from some mangrove swamps on the south coast of Castro's native Oriente Province. The site was more than a mile (1.6km) from Las Coloradas beach, their intended destination. Juan Manuel Márquez claimed, "It wasn't a landing, it was a shipwreck."[49]

The Granma, a small, rickety ship that carried Castro and his rebel forces from Mexico to Cuba to launch their invasion in December 1956, was named a National Historic Shrine by Castro's government.

Castro and his men had to leave most of their supplies on the *Granma* because the ship was stuck far from shore. In fact, it was difficult for the invaders just to force their way to solid ground through the swamp's muck and water.

Batista Strikes at Castro

Three days later at dawn on December 5, Castro and his men stopped to rest in a sugarcane field near the small community of Alegría de Pío. They were hungry because they had almost no food, and they were exhausted after traveling 22 miles (35km) over rough terrain since their landing. They slept, woke up about 4 P.M., and began eating. While they were still consuming their meager rations, more than one hundred soldiers opened fire on them with machine guns and rifles. "Our group was completely surprised,"[50] Castro admitted years later.

Castro's own arrogance was partially to blame for the attack, which nearly ended his attempt to oust Batista. In November, he had sent a statement to the Cuban newspaper *Alerta* boasting that he would invade Cuba in two weeks if Batista did not resign. The threat had put Batista on the alert for an invasion, and he concentrated his search on Oriente Province because it was the area Martí had used in 1895. The dictator learned Castro had landed only a few hours after the *Granma* ran aground because two ships saw the stranded vessel and reported it to officials. Batista ordered military units including airplanes to search the surrounding area and they finally located the invaders.

Cuban troops assemble for transport to the region of eastern Cuba where Castro's rebel forces were hiding following their invasion in December 1956.

Fidel the Dreamer

Alberto Bayo, who helped train Castro's invasion force, recalls:

> The young man [Castro] was telling me that he expected to defeat Batista in a future landing that he planned to carry out with men "when I have them," and with vessels "when I have the money to buy them," because at the moment he was talking to me, he had neither a man nor a dollar. Wasn't it amusing.

Quoted in Tad Szulc, *Fidel: A Critical Portrait*. New York: William Morrow, 1986, pp. 235–236.

The rebels were taken by surprise when the soldiers attacked. "Suddenly," Guevara wrote years later, "there was a steady burst of fire. Bullets whistled right and left. Airplanes appeared and began strafing us."[51] Guevara was hit by a bullet but suffered only minor wounds to the neck and throat. Only three men died in the initial attack, as the others quickly ran for cover from the withering gunfire from both soldiers and airplanes. Castro fled into a sugarcane field with Universo Sánchez and Faustino Pérez. While they hid, jet planes strafed the area around them. Castro remembered that "the earth would shake under the firepower of the .50-caliber machine guns that each jet carried."[52]

When it became dark, Castro and his two companions slipped away from the soldiers who were searching for them. It took them until December 16 to reach a prearranged rendezvous point, a farm on the slopes of the Sierra Maestra range. In the next few days Raúl and four more men arrived and then a third group of rebels including Guevara. Only three of Castro's men died in the initial attack, but fifty-three more had either been killed or captured by soldiers since then.

Castro Vows to Keep Fighting

Castro's invasion had been a disaster, leaving him with only sixteen men to challenge Batista, who led an army of thousands of soldiers. Equally as big a failure was a series of attacks members of the 26th of July Movement staged in conjunction with Castro's arrival. On November 30, groups directed by Frank País—who had led the group in Cuba while Castro was in exile—again attacked the Moncada Barracks and several other military targets. But the army and police easily beat back the assaults, which were designed to ignite a popular uprising that Castro could lead when he got to Cuba.

Castro, however, was not dismayed by either failure. On December 25, he wrote that his group was "about to set out again on our march toward the Sierra Maestra, where we shall go on fighting until we meet with victory or death."[53] They headed into the mountains that Christmas Day to ignite a revolt that would, against all odds, topple Batista and bring Castro to power in his native land.

Chapter 4

Castro Brings Revolution to Cuba

Cuban dictator Fulgencio Batista was so confident his soldiers had eliminated Fidel Castro's small invasion force that in early December 1956 he announced that Castro was dead. Newspapers reported his claim and for more than two months only a handful of Castro's supporters in Cuba knew the truth. But on February 24, 1957, a story appeared on the front page of the *New York Times* under this headline: "Castro Is Still Alive and Still Fighting in Mountains." Reporter Herbert L. Matthews wrote: "This is the first sure news that Fidel Castro is still alive and still in Cuba. No one connected with the outside world, let alone with the press, has seen Señor Castro except this writer. No one in Havana, not even at the United States Embassy with its resources for getting information, will know until this report is published that Fidel Castro is really in the Sierra Maestra."[54]

The article was based on interviews Matthews conducted with Castro in the Sierra Maestra. Castro arranged the meeting with the respected journalist because he wanted the world to know he was alive and fighting Batista. The series of articles Matthews wrote were complimentary to Castro and claimed he had a chance to win his battle. The stories printed in one of the world's most influential newspapers gave Castro's Cuban Revolution a legitimacy it had never previously enjoyed. One reason for the reporter's prediction of success was that the rebel leader had already scored several small victories over Batista's army.

Castro, center, and his team of rebel commanders assemble at their base in the Sierra Maestra mountains in March 1957. Castro's brother Raúl kneels in the foreground; Ernesto "Che" Guevara stands second from left.

"Los Barbudos"

Castro's first successful military action was a response to two pressing needs—supplies for his men and a victory to boost their morale after the disastrous landing. On January 17, Castro attacked a small military facility near La Plata River. Striking at night, his men surprised fifteen Cuban soldiers, killing two of them and wounding five more while suffering no casualties. "That was our first victorious encounter, the first small but symbolic victory,"[55] Castro later wrote. He and his small band obtained food, weapons, medicine, ammunition, and other items they needed after having lost most of their supplies when the *Granma* ran aground. Five days later, the rebels triumphed again when they ambushed a platoon of soldiers searching for them.

The victories raised the spirits of Castro's men and convinced many Cubans who also opposed Batista that Castro could defeat him. New recruits for Castro's small band of rebels began trekking into the Sierra Maestra, a chain of mountains 90 miles (144km) long and 30 miles (48km) wide and covered by dense rain forest. The mountain chain's rugged terrain sheltered Castro from Batista's army between attacks.

The night raid on La Plata set the pattern for Castro's guerrilla war against Batista. His men would strike groups of soldiers or military facilities in lightning-quick assaults. and then return to the safety of their mountain sanctuary. The attacks demoralized Batista's army, cheered Castro's supporters, and secured needed supplies. The rebels moved constantly between raids to avoid capture and aerial bombing attacks. They usually slept on the ground under plastic sheets and wore olive-green fatigues to camouflage themselves in the dense jungle. They also grew heavy beards that gave them the nickname "los barbudos" (the bearded ones).

An Important Interview

New York Times reporter Herbert L. Matthews has been called "the man who invented Fidel Castro" because his stories in 1957 introduced Castro to the world. Matthews describes Castro the first time they met:

[He was] a powerful six-footer, olive-skinned, full-faced, with a straggly beard. He was dressed in an olive gray fatigue uniform and carried a rifle with a telescopic sight, of which he was very proud. "We can pick them [the enemy] off at a thousand yards with these guns," he said. [No] one could talk above a whisper at any time. There were columns of [soldiers] all around us, Señor Castro said ... and their one hope was to catch him and his band. The personality of the man is overpowering. It was easy to see that his men adored him and also to see why he has caught the imagination of the youth of Cuba all over the island. Here was an educated, dedicated fanatic, a man of ideals, of courage and of remarkable qualities of leadership.

Herbert L. Matthews, "Cuban Rebel Is Visited in Hideout, Castro Is Still Alive and Still Fighting in Mountains," New York Times, February 24, 1957, p. 1.

Matthews wrote that "Fidel Castro and his 26th of July Movement are the flaming symbol of opposition to the [Batista] regime."[56] However, he also noted that they were not the only ones fighting the dictator.

Castro Was Not Alone

Many other Cubans hated Batista because his corrupt government favored his rich friends and ignored the needs of the poor. They were also angry that Batista harshly repressed anyone who opposed him politically; soldiers and police jailed, tortured, and murdered thousands of Cubans who had challenged Batista's rule. His opponents included members of the Partido Ortodoxo (Orthodox Party), the Directorio Revolucionario (Revolutionary Directorate), an underground student group, and Cuban exiles such as former president Prío.

In March 1957, the Directorio Revolucionario attacked the National Palace in Havana in a bold but misguided attempt to kill Batista. The poorly armed students were easily defeated. Two months later, a group of exiles funded by Prío landed on Oriente Province to fight Batista but were killed or captured when someone betrayed them to Batista's government. In September, sailors backing Castro revolted against Batista at a naval base in Cienfuegos, but the Cuban military quickly quelled their rebellion. Other groups and individuals opposed to Batista tried to disrupt the Cuban economy. They damaged transportation systems, electric power facilities, and oil refineries and burned sugarcane fields; the last tactic was effective because Cuba's main source of revenue was the sale of sugar to other countries.

Led by Frank País, members of Castro's 26th of July Movement were responsible for many of the attacks. When police killed País in Santiago de Cuba on July 30, 1957, workers who sympathized with Castro went on strike. The labor unrest showed the growing support many Cubans had for Castro. Another sign of the growing unity of Cubans against Batista had come two weeks earlier on July 12 when Castro, Ortodoxo leader Raúl Chibás, and Felipe Pazos, another Batista opponent, issued the Sierra

Maestra Manifesto. The document was a call for all Cubans to fight Batista: "The time has come when the nation can save itself from tyranny through the intelligence, courage, and civic spirit of its children, through the efforts of all those who feel deeply the destiny of this land where we have the right to live in peace and freedom."[57]

In the manifesto, Castro promised to hold elections after he ousted Batista and restore the 1940 Constitution, which ensured Cubans basic civil rights but which Batista had suspended. The growing hatred of Batista and the belief Castro would restore democracy won him many more supporters.

Castro's Army Grows

By October 1957, Castro had nearly two hundred men under his command, a force big enough to defend the Sierra Maestra from attacks and allow him to establish a permanent base camp. He assigned the task of setting up the facility to Che Guevara. Guevara had become one of Castro's most trusted officers by proving himself adept as a military leader.

Argentine revolutionary Ernesto "Che" Guevara, right, helped Castro plan his military strategy and gain the support of ordinary Cubans as the rebel forces battled government troops for control of territory surrounding their mountain base.

Guevara set up a camp that included a barracks, hospital, bakery, and a radio station and newspaper to disseminate news and propaganda to Cubans. The facilities also became part of Castro's attempt to help poor Cubans. Castro fed hungry local residents and Guevara treated their illnesses. Guevara explained why they did that: "We began to feel in our flesh and blood, the need for a definitive change in the life of the people."[58] As Castro won control of more territory surrounding his mountain refuge, he also began giving poor farmers land that he seized from wealthy Cubans and U.S.-owned businesses.

Those tactics helped build support for the Cuban Revolution, and by the middle of 1958 Castro's forces controlled most of Oriente Province even though he had only about three hundred armed men compared with Batista's army of more than forty thousand. The Cuban army, however, was ineffective due to poor leadership and the reluctance many soldiers had to fight Castro because they supported what he was doing to help poor people.

Batista finally realized that Castro posed a real threat to his regime. In May 1958 he launched Fin de Fidel (the end of Fidel), a major offensive to destroy the rebels.

Castro Ousts Batista

On May 20, more than ten thousand soldiers surrounded the Sierra Maestra and began closing in on Castro's headquarters in La Plata. Castro's small force, however, withstood the powerful offensive. His men defeated Batista's soldiers in battle after battle, and the army finally gave up and retreated. The army failed because Castro outmaneuvered the Cuban officers and because most soldiers did not want to fight him. Hundreds of soldiers, sometimes entire units, deserted to join Castro. Their numbers swelled Castro's army to nine hundred, and their weapons made the rebels better armed than ever. On August 20, Castro triumphantly announced on his radio station that the offensive meant to destroy him had instead made him strong enough to conquer Cuba: "After 76 days of unceasing fighting, the Rebel army has

With a defeated Batista taking refuge in the Dominican Republic, Castro triumphantly rides into Havana in January 1959, promising the cheering crowds that the revolution would improve the lives of Cuban citizens.

clearly repulsed and virtually destroyed the cream of the forces of the tyranny. More than thirty clashes and six large-scale battles have taken place. The rebel columns will advance in every direction toward the rest of the territory of the nation and no one will be able to stop them."[59]

Three columns of men commanded by Guevara, Jaime Vega, and Camilo Cienfuegos soon seized control of central Cuba from Batista's dispirited, beaten troops. As Castro's forces advanced, they were joined by thousands of Cubans who wanted Batista ousted from power. In the next few months, the rebel force stormed across Cuba. The climactic battle was fought December 29–31, when three hundred rebels led by Guevara won control of Santa Clara and captured an army garrison of twenty-five hundred soldiers.

Santa Clara and other rebel victories made Batista realize his defeat was inevitable. At 2 A.M. on January 1, 1959, he fled to the Dominican Republic, which was ruled by Rafael Trujillo, another dictator. Castro was now in control of Cuba. The next day he entered Santiago de Cuba, which had surrendered following Batista's departure. In a speech to a cheering crowd, Castro promised to make changes that would help Cubans have better lives: "The Revolution begins now. The Revolution will not be an easy task. The Revolution will be a very difficult undertaking full of danger. The Revolution [means that] for the first time the republic will really be entirely free and the people will have what they deserve. This was won by the people!"[60]

When Castro entered Havana on January 8, residents of Cuba's capital city turned out to cheer him. They welcomed him because he had promised to help the poor, end political repression, and eliminate government corruption. Castro that day declared, "Now, we are going to purify this country."[61] The first step in that process would mean the deaths of hundreds of Castro's former opponents.

The Bearded Ones

The story of our beards is very simple: it arose out of the difficult conditions we were living and fighting under as guerrillas. We didn't have any razor blades, or straight razors. When we found ourselves in the middle of the wilderness, up in the Sierra [Maestra], everybody just let their beards and hair grow, and that turned into a kind of badge of identity. For the campesinos [poor farmers who lived nearby] and everybody else, for the press, for the reporters we were "los barbudos"— the bearded ones. It had its positive side: in order for a spy to infiltrate us, he had to start preparing months ahead of time—he'd have had to have a six-months growth of beard, you see. So the beards served as a badge of identification, and as protection, until it finally became a symbol of the guerrilla fighter. Later, with the triumph of the Revolution, we kept our beards to preserve the symbolism.

Fidel Castro and Ignacio Ramonet, *Fidel Castro: My Life*. New York: Scribner, 2008, p. 195.

A Brutal Beginning

In the first few weeks after Castro took control of Cuba, his government arrested, tried, and punished thousands of government and military officials from Batista's regime. Most of the officials the rebels tried had cruelly imprisoned, tortured, and murdered Castro's supporters and other people who opposed Batista. Castro's new government executed about 550 people for such acts. Their deaths were legal only because Castro's new government legalized capital punishment, which Cuba had previously banned.

Many people in Cuba and other countries criticized the trials because they were conducted so quickly and informally that no one believed justice could have been done. U.S. ambassador Philip W. Bonsal noted that on January 5 in Santiago de Cuba "some 70 prisoners were mowed down by rebel soldiers [and] bulldozed under the ground without any semblance of a trial."[62] Raúl Castro was the officer in charge of that brutal mass execution.

Castro's government also punished soldiers who fought against him. When forty-three members of the Cuban air force were found innocent of charges connected with bombing the rebels, Castro ordered a retrial. They were found guilty and sentenced to thirty years in prison. Many people thought it was cruel to punish soldiers who had only been doing their duty by fighting someone who was trying to overthrow their government. Castro years later claimed the rebels acted in a just manner in how it punished former Batista officials and soldiers: "We don't regret having done it. We created tribunals that carried out traditional trials and punished those who'd committed war crimes."[63]

The brutality that Castro's regime showed toward its former enemies shocked and angered many people around the world. So did the way Castro began to reshape Cuba's economy.

Castro Changes Cuba

The United States recognized Castro's new government on January 7. President Dwight D. Eisenhower allowed it, even though he was still concerned Castro might be a Communist—his greatest

Cuban women tend to a plot of land seized by Castro's government in accordance with the Agrarian Reform Act of 1959, which outlawed the ownership of land by wealthy citizens and foreigners and created farming cooperatives.

fear was to have a Communist nation close enough to attack the United States. Castro temporarily eased those concerns in April 1959 when he made a fifteen-day visit to the United States. In several public appearances, Castro stated he was not a Communist and wanted friendly relations with the United States: "I have said in a clear and definitive fashion that we are not Communists. The doors are open to private investments that contribute to the industrial development of Cuba. It is absolutely impossible for us to make progress if we do not come to an understanding with the United States."[64]

But when Castro returned to Cuba, he instituted sweeping changes that made those statements seem like lies. On May 17, 1959, Castro signed into law an agrarian reform act that prohibited individuals from owning more than 993 acres of land and foreigners from owning any land. The law allowed the government to seize land from wealthy individuals, U.S. firms like United Fruit, and even Castro's parents. The government gave small plots of the land to poor Cubans to farm. The government also took over electric companies, oil refineries, and other large companies. In a crackdown on vice in Havana, Cuba seized and shut down hotels and gambling casinos that U.S. crime figures owned.

Castro, who was now Cuba's prime minister, was acting like a Communist when he did such things. Communism is an economic doctrine that claims the government, not individuals, should own and control agricultural land, factories, and businesses so that the profits they create can benefit all citizens and not just a few individuals. Castro's actions put his government at odds with the United States, which as a capitalist nation believes individuals have the right to own property and become rich.

Guevera and Raúl Castro, who were both Communists, heavily influenced Castro in making those changes. But Castro claims he was still not a Communist when he imposed them on Cuba, only a Marxist. Karl Marx was the German philosopher who originated Communist principles. Marx claimed that history has been a continuous struggle between rich and poor people. Castro believed that theory from reading Marx and from his own experience as a child, when he felt it was unfair that poor children he played with did not have shoes and often went hungry. Castro's goal in reshaping Cuba's economy was to help more people have a decent life. During his visit to the United States in April he told one reporter, "We do hope to raise the standard of living of everyone to what the middle class now has."[65]

Eisenhower and U.S. officials, however, believed Castro was setting Cuba on the path to communism. That made Cuba a Cold War enemy.

The Soviets Befriend Castro

During the Cold War, both the United States and the USSR used economic aid to win the support of other countries. Realizing there was a chance to make Cuba an ally in this conflict, the Soviets moved to establish an economic connection with Cuba. On February 13, 1960, the two nations signed an economic pact in which the Soviets agreed to buy hundreds of tons of sugar and gave Cuba a $100 million low-interest loan to buy oil, wheat, and other commodities it needed. The USSR also promised to send technical experts to help Cuba build new factories and make other technological improvements. Castro said, "The agreement is a good one and favorable to Cuba in every aspect. We are going to be a rich little country."[66]

The Eisenhower administration was already angry at Cuba because Castro had seized more than $3.3 billion in property owned by U.S. individuals and businesses. The pact linking Cuba with the Soviets made the president angry enough to want to punish Cuba. On March 17, 1960, he signed an order authorizing funds to train Cuban exiles living in the United States who

Castro and Soviet leader Nikita Khrushchev, right, forged an economic partnership between their nations in 1960, a move that stoked Cold War tensions and prompted the United States to step up its efforts to oust Castro from power.

A U.S. Official Comments on Executions

Central Intelligence Agency director Allen Dulles comments on executions following the Cuban Revolution's victory in 1959:

When you have a revolution, you kill your enemies. There were many instances of cruelty and repression by the Cuban army, and they [the new rebel government] had the goods on some of those people. Now there will probably be a lot of justice. It will probably go much too far, but they have to go through with this.

Quoted in Robert E. Quirk, *Fidel Castro*. New York: Norton, 1993, p. 225.

opposed Castro and wanted to invade Cuba and oust Castro from power as he had Batista. That was a long-range plan to harm Castro. On July 6, Eisenhower moved to immediately weaken Cuba economically by banning sugar imports from Cuba, which got most of its revenue from such sales.

Three days later the USSR promised to buy the Cuban sugar that the United States no longer wanted. Soviet premier Nikita Khrushchev announced the deal, saying, "The U.S.S.R is raising its voice and extending a helpful hand to the people of Cuba. Speaking figuratively, in case of necessity, Soviet artillerymen can support the Cuban people with rocket fire."[67] Khruschev was being overly dramatic in saying his nation would protect Cuba in case the United States attacked it, but his words further escalated tensions between Cuba and the United States. Eisenhower responded on October 19 by prohibiting any U.S. aid to Cuba in the form of food, medicine, or medical supplies; that decision marked the beginning of a U.S. economic blockade against Cuba that continued for decades.

Cubans Flee Castro

The drastic changes that Castro made and the violence that accompanied the birth of his new regime led many people to flee Cuba. In the first five years after Castro seized power an estimated one million Cubans, almost 10 percent of the island's population, immigrated to the United States. They included former government officials and even Castro's own sister, Juanita. Many of the expatriate Cubans soon began working, as Castro once had, to overthrow what they believed was a brutal dictator in their former homeland.

Chapter 5

Castro Versus the United States

Fidel Castro grew up admiring America's power and riches, and in 1940 the fourteen-year-old Castro even wrote a friendly letter to President Franklin D. Roosevelt. But as an adult Castro came to resent the economic and political control the United States wielded over his homeland. And when Castro was trying to overthrow Fulgencio Batista, the United States became his enemy because it gave Batista weapons to fight against Castro. In June 1958, Castro wrote how angry he was that U.S.-supplied missiles had destroyed the home of a supporter: "When I saw the rockets that they fired on Mario's house, I swore that the Americans are going to pay dearly for what they're doing. When this war is over, I'll start a much longer and bigger war of my own: the war I'm going to fight against them. I realize that will be my true destiny."[68] It would only take a few years for Castro to start fulfilling that destiny.

The United States Opposes Castro

Castro denied he was a Communist the first two years he ruled Cuba. But U.S. president Dwight D. Eisenhower considered Castro a Cold War enemy anyway due to Cuba's close ties to the Soviet Union and its economic policy of seizing U.S.-owned assets. On January 3, 1961, Eisenhower finally severed diplomatic relations with Cuba. "There is a limit to what the United States in self-respect can endure," he said. "That limit has now

Castro Interrogates Prisoners

On April 27, 1961, Fidel Castro questioned Cuban exiles captured during the Bay of Pigs invasion. The interrogation was broadcast on radio by Havana Domestic Service. Castro told the men that they should be ashamed the botched invasion had been planned and funded by the Central Intelligence Agency (CIA) and approved by President John F. Kennedy:

> Castro asked the prisoners if they knew that the United States had organized the invasion, then read excerpts from [two U.S. publications]. These things, he said, were not said by a Cuban paper but by *Time* [magazine] and the *New York Post* [newspaper]. He asked the prisoners [if] they were ashamed that they had been merely puppets [of the United States]. He asked them to remember how different had been the struggle of his small group of men who had faith in the people, who knew they defended a just cause. "Are you not indignant that they admit now that the CIA organized this expedition and that Kennedy gave the order and that the leaders of the invasion did not even know when their sons were coming?" he asked.

"Fidel Castro Interrogates Invasion Prisoners." Castro Speech Data Base, Latin American Network Information Center (LANIC) at the University of Texas. http://www1.lanic.utexas.edu/project/castro/db/1961/19610427.html.

been reached."[69] His announcement came a day after two incidents offended him. On January 2, a Cuban spokesman charged during a United Nations meeting that the United States wanted to invade Cuba. The Cuban army that same day paraded through Havana with tanks, rocket launchers, and other weapons the Soviets had given Cuba.

Eisenhower's anger over Cuba's UN accusation was a sham because the United States was backing an attempted invasion. The president on March 17, 1960, had approved a wide-ranging Central Intelligence Agency (CIA) plan to try to remove Castro from power. The most significant action the CIA took was to provide funding and training for Cuban exiles who wanted to invade Cuba and overthrow Castro. Before the invasion force was ready, however, Eisenhower was succeeded by John F. Kennedy, who was elected president on November 8, 1960. In his inaugural address on January 20, 1961, Kennedy boldly proclaimed he would act forcefully against any country that opposed the United States: "Let every nation know, whether it wishes us well or ill, that we shall pay any price, bear any burden, meet any hardship, support any friend, oppose any foe, to assure the survival and the success of liberty."[70]

Kennedy's warning was aimed at the nation's Cold War enemies, which now included Cuba. Three months later, Kennedy backed up his threat by allowing the exiles to invade Cuba.

Castro Crushes the Invaders

A force of about fifteen hundred men known as Brigade 2506 had trained for months in Guatemala. On April 14, 1961, they left Puerto Cabezas, Nicaragua, in six ships bound for Bahia de Cochina (Bay of Pigs), which was located on Cuba's southern coast 100 miles (160km) southeast of Havana. At 2 A.M. on April 17, the exiles began wading ashore at two beaches, Playa Girón and Playa Larga. The invasion came less than five years after Castro himself had invaded Cuba in a similar mission.

The invasion failed because the exiles were quickly attacked by Cuban soldiers. Cuban officials had learned an invasion was being planned, and Castro himself had scouted the island for possible invasion sites. When Castro visited the Bay of Pigs, he realized it was a likely invasion spot and stationed soldiers there. Once the invasion began, more troops flooded the area and within three days defeated Brigade 2506. A few hundred invaders escaped back to their ships but the Cuban army killed more than a hundred men and took 1,189 prisoners. On April 20, Castro announced Cuba's military victory on Havana Union Radio: "The revolution has been victorious, although it paid with a high number of courageous lives of revolutionary fighters, and faced the invaders and attacked them incessantly without a single minute of truce, thereby destroying in less than 72 hours the army the U.S. imperialist government had organized for many months. The enemy has suffered a crushing defeat."[71]

The CIA had hoped the exiles would spark a popular uprising against Castro. Instead, the botched invasion gave Castro a military triumph that made him a hero to Cubans for standing up to the powerful United States. He gained another victory over the United States in December when it gave Cuba $53 million in medicine, baby food, and other supplies to free the captured exiles.

Castro's forces pose triumphantly in a launch used by Cuban exiles backed by the United States during the Bay of Pigs invasion in April 1961.

Castro's successes gave rise to a popular song, "Cuba Si, Yanquis No," which denounced the United States and helped turn Cubans against their powerful neighbor. U.S. involvement in the invasion also pushed Castro closer to a full-scale alliance with the Communists. Castro had wanted to remain friendly with the United States in hopes that the relationship could benefit Cuba economically. But because tensions between the nations remained high throughout 1961, Castro realized he had no choice but to depend on Communist countries for economic help. In a radio address on January 2, 1962, Castro defiantly declared he was a Communist. "We chose the only honorable path," Castro said. "I say here with complete satisfaction and confidence that I am a [Communist], and shall remain so till the last days of my life."[72]

In a few more months, Cuba's new status as a Soviet ally would ignite the most frightening incident in the decades-long Cold War struggle between Communist and democratic nations.

Cuba Gets Nuclear Missiles

The Bay of Pigs invasion made Castro believe Cuba was vulnerable to future attacks by the United States. Soviet leader Nikita Khrushchev took advantage of that fear to persuade Castro to allow him to place a nuclear missile base in Cuba. He said the missiles would be a deterrent to U.S. aggression because they could strike major U. S. cities, including Washington, D.C., the nation's capital. Khrushchev's real motive in placing the missiles in Cuba, however, was to achieve nuclear balance with its Cold War foe. The United States already had nuclear missiles in Europe and Turkey that could hit the Soviet Union. Castro later said that he had no choice but to accept the missiles from his Cold War protector: "I thought if we expected the Soviets to fight for us, to take risks for us, and if they were even prepared to go to war for our sake, it would have been immoral not to allow the presence of the missiles here."[73]

A Soviet ship arrived in Cuba on September 8 with the first shipment of forty missiles. On October 14 a U.S. spy plane took photographs that showed construction was underway in Cuba on a nuclear missile site. President Kennedy was deeply troubled

An October 1962 spy photo shows the presence of Soviet nuclear weapons and related equipment and structures at a ballistic missile base in Cuba, a discovery that brought the U.S. and the U.S.S.R. to the brink of nuclear war.

when he learned that missiles that could harm the United States were being placed in Cuba. In the next few days, Kennedy met with high-ranking officials and advisers to decide what to do about the missiles. "We must bring the [nuclear] threat to an end," Kennedy told them. "One way or another, the missiles must go."[74] The options Kennedy considered included a full-scale invasion and even a nuclear attack to destroy the site.

The president kept news about the missiles secret until October 22, when he explained the situation in a televised speech. Kennedy announced that the Soviets had placed nuclear weapons in Cuba that could target major U.S. cities and boldly demanded that the Soviets remove them. He said that to prevent deliveries of more missiles, 180 ships were being positioned around Cuba. The U.S. Navy would search any ships headed for Cuba to make sure no more weapons got through. In addition, U.S. troops and planes were massing on the nation's southeast coast for possible further military action.

Kennedy's speech stunned and frightened people around the world because they believed the disagreement could lead to nuclear war. Many historians believe the missile crisis was the most dangerous event in history because of fears that a nuclear war could destroy the world.

The Cuban Missile Crisis

Castro was alarmed by the defiant tone of Kennedy's speech and worried about a possible nuclear war; years later, Castro admitted that he believed then that there was one chance in three that the incident could ignite nuclear war. But Castro was also proud that his small country was showing the world it was brave enough to stand up to the powerful United States. In an interview years later, Castro said, "For the first time we were participating in a certain state of equality with an enemy that had been attacking and provoking us incessantly, and we were really enjoying such a different and new situation."[75]

President John F. Kennedy leaves St. Stephen's Roman Catholic Church in Washington, D.C. on October 28, 1962, shortly after the announcement from Moscow that Khrushchev removed rocket missiles from Cuba. In return, the United States promised not to attack Cuba.

Even though the world's attention was centered on Cuba, it was Kennedy and Khrushchev who had to resolve the crisis. The same night Kennedy gave his speech, he sent a message to the Soviet leader explaining his demand and informing Khrushchev about the quarantine. A convoy of eighteen Soviet ships believed to be carrying nuclear weapons was headed for Cuba, and as they neared the blockade the world waited to see what would happen. All but one ship turned back before reaching the cordon of U.S. ships. As U.S. defense secretary Dean Rusk said when that

Castro and Angola

On November 4, 1975, Fidel Castro ordered the deployment of hundreds of Cuban soldiers to the African nation of Angola. They helped the Communist Popular Movement for the Liberation of Angola win control of that country in a bitter civil war. Gabriel García Márquez, the Nobel Prize-winning novelist from Colombia, is a close friend of Castro. Márquez claims Castro was personally committed to the fight in Angola:

> He saw off all the ships, and before each departure he gave a pep talk to the soldiers [heading to Angola]. He personally had picked up the commanders of the battalion of special forces that left in the first flight and had driven them himself in his Soviet jeep to the foot of the plane ramp. [Castro had] a deep sentiment of envy for those going off to a war that he could not participate in. There was no spot on the map of Angola that he couldn't identify or a physical feature that he hadn't memorized. He could quote any figure on Angola as if it were Cuba, and he spoke of Angolan cities, customs, and people as if he had lived there his entire life.

Georgie Anne Geyer, *Guerrilla Prince: The Untold Story of Fidel Castro.* Boston: Little Brown, 1991, p. 347.

happened, "We're eyeball to eyeball and I think the other fellows just blinked."[76] The Soviets had backed down from the threat of war with the United States.

On October 26, Khrushchev sent a proposal to Kennedy saying the Soviet Union would remove the missiles if the United States promised not to attack Cuba and if it would remove U.S. missiles it had in Turkey. Kennedy agreed to the compromise to end the deadly impasse.

The peaceful resolution to the crisis pleased almost everyone in the world except Castro. He did not find out about the agreement until October 28, when he heard it on the radio because the Soviet Union never told the Cubans it was negotiating with the United States. Castro was angry the Soviets had ignored him and his nation while making decisions that affected Cuba. In a 1992 interview, Castro explained why he had been furious: "Not only was this decision taken without consulting us, several steps [in the crisis] were taken without informing us. So we were humiliated."[77]

Castro, however, had no choice but to allow the Soviets to remove the missiles he had wanted as protection against the United States. That was because by turning Communist, Castro had made his nation economically dependent upon the Soviet Union. The arrangement would have both positive and negative effects on life in Cuba.

Communist Cuba

On January 2, 1967, a story by reporter Herbert L. Matthews appeared in the *New York Times* that described how Cuba had changed in the eight years since Castro had come to power. Matthews wrote that Communist rule had made life better for many people:

There have been improvements in child care, public health, housing, roads and the typical leveling down of the whole social and economic structure that accompanies revolutionary "equality." This also means, however, that the poorest

Workers harvest sugar cane, a crop that dominated the Cuban economy in the 1960s despite Castro's desire to diversify industry in his nation.

and most backward elements, especially in the rural areas, have been "leveled up." Cuban Negroes, for the first time, have equal status with whites, economically and socially.[78]

In Communist Cuba, the government owned and operated almost all businesses and everyone worked for the government. Wages were tiny compared with those in capitalist nations, but people did not need as much money because the government provided low-cost housing and free services such as health care and education. Poor people, who were in the majority, lived better than in the past while those who had been well-off or wealthy had a reduced living standard. Tens of thousands of rich people left Cuba as did doctors, lawyers, and other educated people because they believed they could have a better life in a non-Communist nation.

Cuba's standard of living, however, depended on the strength of its economy. For decades, about three-fourths of the money Cuba's economy produced had come from sugar. Castro wanted to end dependence on one crop by developing industries that could produce consumer products that Cuba had to buy from other countries. His dream of economic self-sufficiency, however, was killed by Cuba's alliance with the Soviet Union.

Castro had initially hoped to get funding from the U.S. government and U.S. businesses to build up Cuba's economy. But the United States, once Cuba's main economic partner, rejected Castro's overtures for help and even quit buying sugar because it considered Cuba a Cold War foe. And in February 1963, the Kennedy administration began an economic embargo against Cuba that made it illegal for citizens to travel to Cuba or have any financial and commercial transactions with the island nation.

Cuba had to continue to rely on sugar for most of its revenue because the Soviet Union forced it to grow as much as it could to supply the Communist countries it controlled. Cuba's economy at times was weaker than ever under this arrangement because the Soviets set the price they paid for sugar in return for economic aid and consumer products. As a result, Cuba sometimes did not have enough money to buy what it needed. In 1968 Cuba rationed gasoline because the Soviet Union reduced its supply, and in 1969 Cuba had to ration even sugar because so much had to be given to the Soviets.

Castro Spreads Communism

The Soviet refusal to challenge the United States during the missile crisis made Castro believe its leaders were too timid in opposing capitalist nations. Castro wanted to be more aggressive than the Soviets in spreading communism. He believed it was the best system to ensure that everyone had a decent life. In 1966 he said, "What we are convinced about is that in the immense majority of Latin American nations conditions exist for making the [Communist] Revolution that are far superior to those that existed in Cuba, and that if those revolutions are not being made in those countries it is because many who call themselves revolutionaries lack conviction."[79]

Ernesto "Che" Guevara, who had helped Castro defeat Batista, was also convinced other countries needed to become Communist. In March 1965, Castro gave Guevara permission to take 120 Cuban soldiers to the Congo to help a Communist group win control of that African nation, which is known today as the Democratic Republic of the Congo. Guevara and his men fought unsuccessfully for several months before returning home. Guevara tried again in 1967 when he took a small force of Cubans to Bolivia to start a Communist revolution. That failed also, and he was captured and executed by Bolivian soldiers.

Castro kept supporting Communist revolutionaries in Latin America and Africa. In the 1970s, Castro helped Communists win control of Nicaragua in Central America and Angola in Africa, the latter victory involving nearly forty thousand Cuban soldiers in a bitter war involving several nations. Castro's commitment to spread communism in countries like Angola in the decades after the missile crisis continued to make him an enemy of the United States. Conditions in Cuba also made him hated by some of his own people.

Ernesto "Che" Guevara poses with a child and a soldier in the Congo, where he and 120 Cuban troops traveled in 1965 with Castro's blessing to support a Communist insurgency in that African nation.

Castro Tightens Control of Cuba

The [Bay of Pigs] fiasco allowed Castro to consolidate his power and pushed him further into the arms of the Soviets. In December 1961, he boldly declared an outright alliance with the Soviet Union, at which point Soviet Premier Nikita Khrushchev warned that he would defend Cuba against American aggression, even to the point of nuclear war.

Charles Phillips, "April 17, 1961: Bay of Pigs Invasion," *American History*, p. 18.

Political Repression

Shortages of food, vital commodities such as gasoline, and consumer products due to Cuba's continuing weak economy made life unpleasant or even difficult for many people. Added to this dissatisfaction was the lack of political freedom in Cuba. The Communist Party was the only one that Castro allowed to exist, and anyone who disagreed with Communist ideas or government actions was punished.

Gerardo Sanchez, whose brother Elizardo was imprisoned for two years for speaking against government policies, explained in 1990 that "if you lift your head, they cut it off. So you keep your head down. But that doesn't mean your brain doesn't work."[80] Sanchez meant that Cubans are so fearful of their government that they keep quiet even when they disagree with it. They have to do this because Cuba is a police state. In addition to being watched by police and military intelligence officers, Cubans are spied on at home by government observers; one is placed on every city block, in every rural area, and at school by the Union of Young Communists. Such observers report any statements or actions that might be critical or harmful to the government. Thousands of Cubans have been locked up and even executed for opposing the Castro regime.

Hundreds of thousands of Cubans, including Castro's daughter, Alina Fernández Revuelta, have fled their nation's repressive communist regime. Many of those in exile, including Fernández, have become outspoken critics of the Castro administration.

Communist repression of individual and political freedom has forced hundreds of thousands of Cubans to flee their homeland since Castro took power. The exiles have even included members of Castro's family, including his sister Juanita Castro Ruz. In July 1964, she defected to the United States after visiting her sister Emma in Mexico. Castro's sister said she hated what her brother had done to Cuba: "I cannot longer remain indifferent to what is happening in my country. My brothers Fidel and Raúl have made it an enormous prison surrounded by water. The people are nailed to a cross of torment imposed by international Communism."[81]

Cuban exiles have also included Alina Fernández Revuelta, the illegitimate daughter Castro had with Natalie Revuelta. She was born March 18, 1956, while Castro was in Mexico plotting to oust Batista. Alina escaped Cuba in December 1993 by boarding a plane disguised as a Spanish tourist. A few months later, her sixteen-year-old daughter, Alina Maria, was allowed to join her in the United States.

Castro and Communism Fade in Cuba

I n 1988, Maria Shriver interviewed Fidel Castro for NBC television. Shriver was an ironic choice to question Castro because she was the niece of President John F. Kennedy, Castro's foe in the Bay of Pigs and Cuban Missile Crisis. Castro told Shriver, "We are left with the honor of being one of the few adversaries of the United States." When Shriver asked Castro if he was really proud of being considered her nation's enemy, Castro replied: "Of course it is an honor, because for such a small country as Cuba to have such a gigantic country as the United States live so obsessed with this little island—a country that no longer considers itself an adversary of the USSR or an adversary of [Communist] China, yet still considers itself an adversary of Cuba—it is an honor for us."[82]

The Cold War was nearly over when Castro made that remark. Although the USSR and the People's Republic of China were still Communist, they had resumed peaceful relations with their former Cold War enemy. The United States, however, still considered Cuba a foe. In a few more years, the status Castro boasted about would have disastrous results for his country.

Cuba's "Special Period"

Cuba's economy was fueled for nearly three decades by billions of dollars in economic aid and sugar payments that it received annually from the Soviet Union. The USSR began disintegrating in the

Elián González

Fidel Castro's last big victory over the United States was in 2000 in the political battle over Elián González. On November 25, 1999, the five-year-old boy was rescued from the Atlantic Ocean three miles off the coast of Florida while clinging to an inner tube. He was a survivor of an ill-fated attempt by his mother and fourteen other people to leave Cuba. His mother was one of a dozen people who died when the small boat they were in sank before it reached the United States. Elián and two other people stayed afloat on inner tubes until two fishermen rescued them. His rescue touched off a bitter custody battle between relatives in Florida and his father in Cuba. The fight over Elián became a political tug-of-war between the two old Cold War foes. Castro argued that Elián should be returned to his father and his native country. The boy's relatives claimed that living under communism would hurt him. A federal court finally ruled his father had custody of Elián. When he was returned to Cuba on June 28, 2000, Castro claimed to have beaten the United States—again.

Six-year-old Elián González was found clinging to an inner tube in the Atlantic Ocean after the boat carrying him, his mother, and others to Florida sank. The ensuing custody battle between his relatives in the United States and his father in Cuba became an international story.

late 1980s when Communist nations of Eastern Europe such as Poland and Hungary broke away from it because they rejected communism. By 1991 the Soviet Union no longer existed. The breakup of the Soviet Union meant not only the end of the long Cold War but an end to the economic relationship that had kept Cuba financially solvent. It also marked the beginning of what became known as Cuba's "Special Period in Peacetime (Período Especial en Tiempo de Paz)," an era of financial hardship.

The Special Period began in 1990 and lasted into the mid-1990s. Without Soviet subsidies or markets for its sugar, Cuba's gross domestic product—a term for the money a country's economy produces—fell 35 percent between 1989 and 1993. The drop in Cuba's income produced economic difficulties that included shortages of food, medicine, and consumer items. Cuba became so poor it had to ration gasoline. The fuel shortage meant farmers had to use oxen to plow fields instead of tractors. Cuba also imported a half-million bicycles from China so people could use them for transportation instead of buses. The country also did not have enough money to provide electricity for everyone for the entire day. As a result, different areas of the island were without power each day during scheduled power blackouts.

Cuba had to buy much of the food its people consumed because they could not grow enough food to feed everyone. Food also had to be rationed, which made many people angry. A woman in Havana told a reporter during this period that she worried about babies because canned milk was being rationed. "This is scandalous," she said. "They [officials] think a child can grow up healthy on six cans of milk a month!"[83] As conditions worsened, factories and businesses closed, unemployment climbed, and shortages of many items worsened. Even Castro has admitted that Cubans suffered during this period: "The country took a stunning blow when that great power collapsed and left us out in the cold, all by ourselves, and we lost all our markets for sugar, we stopped receiving foodstuffs, fuel, even the wood [for coffins] to bury our dead in. From one day to the next, we found ourselves without fuel, without raw materials, without food, without soap, without everything."[84]

The economic situation became so bleak that Castro had to

relent slightly on his commitment to communism. Castro allowed countries friendly to Cuba—Canada as well as European and Latin American nations—to make financial investments in Cuba. Much of the money that flowed into Cuba went to build hotels and open businesses such as nightclubs that were associated with tourism. Cuba began to encourage tourism after decades of ignoring the desire of people to visit there. Castro also allowed people to begin operating small businesses, including importing and exporting products, without having to seek government permission.

Castro also strengthened Cuba's economy by allowing Cubans to use U.S. currency to make purchases. This enabled Cuban exiles in the United States to send money to relatives and friends. The resulting flow of hundreds of millions of dollars each year to Cuba strengthened its economy by giving people more money to buy products. Ironically this economic improvement came from people who hated Castro because of what he had done to their island home.

Cubans in Exile

In 2008 more than 2 million Cuban exiles lived in the United States, nearly half of them in the Miami, Florida, area. Cubans began fleeing their homeland as soon as Castro ousted Batista because they feared he was Communist. The exodus continued in the first few years as Castro was transforming Cuba into a Communist nation. One of the most publicized early migrations was Operation Peter Pan (Operacíon Pedro Pan). Between 1960 and 1962, parents who feared they would be punished for opposing Castro sent more than fourteen thousand children to Miami. One of them was thirteen-year-old Florencio Nadal, who became a doctor like his father. Nadal, who lived in Brandon, Florida, explained why his parents feared for his safety: "Castro took everything from my uncle and he was jailed, then my dad was put in jail for trying to help my uncle."[85] Nadal did not see his family until they were allowed to leave Cuba three years later.

Although some Cubans have been escaping Cuba ever since, there have been several periods in which great numbers of people

Cuban refugees aboard a cramped shrimp boat land in Key West, Florida, in April 1980. Tens of thousands of desperate Cubans have attempted the treacherous trip from their island nation to the U.S. mainland in hopes of fleeing Castro's oppressive rule.

fled their homeland. The biggest was the Mariel Boatlift in 1980. Castro became so fed up with Cubans who wanted to leave that he allowed small boats from Miami to come to the port of Mariel and take people back to the United States. More than 125,000 Cubans went to the United States in just a few weeks.

The number of Cubans trying to leave also escalated during the Special Period, when people were so desperate to leave that they tried to float the 90 miles (144km) across the Atlantic Ocean to the United States on small boats or home-made rafts. They became known as "balseros" (rafters) and many of them drowned during the perilous journey when their crafts sank. The dissatisfaction young people felt with the bleak life in Cuba continued to make many risk their lives to leave. From October 2005 through September 2007, an estimated seventy-seven thousand Cubans fled to the United States by any means possible in the largest exodus since the Mariel boatlift. Julia Núñez Pacheco's husband, Adolfo Fernández Sainz, is in prison in Cuba for writing articles critical of the government. "Young people," Pacheco claims, "are

Brayan Peña, left, and Yunel Escobar of the Atlanta Braves are two of several Cubans who play professional baseball in the United States. They are among many Cuban exiles who have achieved prominence and success after escaping Castro's regime.

very fed up with the situation. Many are escaping by hurling themselves into the sea on a raft."[86] Her daughter is one of those who left.

Many Cuban exiles have become successful, politically powerful, and famous. In 2008, Lincoln and Mario Díaz-Balart were Florida congressmen. Their father, Rafael, is the brother of Castro's first wife. Brayan Peña and Yunel Escobar, who both play for the Atlanta Braves, are two of many Cuban professional baseball players. Escobar defected to the United States while playing in an international tournament outside Cuba in 1999 and Peña made the journey by boat in 2004. In what Escobar said "was an amazing experience for us,"[87] they shook hands with President George W. Bush on April 1, 2008, before their season-opener against the Washington Nationals.

Castro has always despised those who left Cuba. He calls them "gusanos" (worms) and claims that "for over forty years, every person who leaves Cuba is an 'exile,' an 'enemy of the Socialist regime.'"[88] Those exiles, however, include his sister Juanita and his only daughter. Since Alina Fernández escaped in 1993, she has been a vocal critic of her father. "I think," she has said, "that my father did a very bad job for Cuba. Cuba is ruined."[89] She has leveled those criticisms in her book *Castro's Daughter* as well as on *Simply Alina,* her program on WQBA, Miami's Cuban-American radio station in Miami.

U.S. Citizens Visit Cuba Illegally

In 2008, the United States still prohibited citizens from visiting Cuba. Even though it was a crime, some Americans did it anyway to see what Cuba was like. U.S. citizens avoided possible punishment by flying to Cuba from Mexico or another foreign country. Cuban officials encourage such visits and do not stamp passports because such tourists help the island's economy. Americans, however, have to make sure officials in another country do not stamp their passports when they return from the visit. An American explains how he and other travelers avoided that problem:

> The tricky part for Americans visiting Cuba is once they leave Cuba and land back in Mexico. At that point, it is important that they not have their passports stamped. If the passport is stamped, it will show them leaving Mexico and then returning to Mexico, but with no stamps from other countries in between. A simple cash bribe of $30 at Mexican customs will insure that the officials do not stamp the passport on re-entry to Mexico from Cuba. And because Cuba does NOT stamp Americans' passports, the U.S. government will not know they visited there.

Interview with the author, April 10, 2008.

For four decades, however, neither the criticism of exiles like his daughter nor attacks by a succession of U.S. presidents have bothered Cuba's *jefe máximo*.

Castro's Private, Public Life

In the decades since Castro took power, he has lived a curious life that was both very public and highly private. Castro has visited countries around the world to spread his message of revolution. He has been especially influential in Latin America, where several generations of leaders such as Venezuelan president Hugo Chavez have deeply admired him. When Castro visited Argentina in 2002, an audience of tens of thousands of people gathered outside the University of Buenos Aires Law School to hear him. After students asked him about Ernesto "Che" Guevara, a native of Argentina, Castro talked for twenty minutes and told them, "There are millions of men like El Che among the masses of Latin America."[90] The young students cheered the elderly revolutionary who was nearly four times their age.

Castro has always loved being in the public eye in his position as Cuba's leader, whether giving speeches that go on for hours, attending conferences around the world, or giving interviews to journalists. Castro has been fanatic, however, about shielding details of his private life from the public. "In this sense," he said, "I have reserved for myself a total freedom."[91]

This secrecy extends to his family. The only child Castro has publicly recognized is his son Fidel Castro Díaz-Balart. Fidel Jr. is a nuclear physicist who has traveled widely outside Cuba to represent it at scientific conferences. But Fidel never mentions Fernández, his only daughter. He also does not acknowledge five sons he has had with Dalia Soto del Valle; they are named Angel, Antonio, Alejandro, Alexis, and Alex. Castro met del Valle, a former schoolteacher, during the literacy campaigns of the 1960s when millions of Cubans learned to read. Although they have been a couple since then, little is known about her, including whether Castro ever married her.

Castro does not even reveal many details about his life to close

Students in Argentina carry a painting of Castro into an auditorium at the law school at the University of Buenos Aires before the Cuban leader's speech there in 2003, which saw tens of thousands of people clamoring to hear his message of revolution.

friends. Gabriel García Márquez, the famed Colombian novelist who won the Nobel Prize in Literature, has known Castro for four decades. Castro has even given him a house near his own in Havana to use during visits. But Márquez has never been to Castro's home and does not even know where it is. He once said of Castro that "he keeps his private life immensely private. He has never introduced me to his wife, for example, or even mentioned her to me. I met her once because one day in Fidel's jet she came up and introduced herself. I don't know that it is true, but people say that Fidel hasn't even introduced [his brother] Raúl to his wife! What is private for him is the most private of private."[92]

The sheltering walls Castro had erected around himself were finally breached in 2006, when he was so ill that he had to be hospitalized.

Castro Relinquishes Power

On July 31, 2006, Cubans were stunned to learn Castro was so ill that he was temporarily naming his brother Raúl as president. The televised announcement caught the nation of 11 million people by surprise even though Castro was eighty years old and had looked increasingly frail in recent years. Castro had ruled so long and survived so many attempts to kill him, including some initiated by U.S. intelligence agencies, that it seemed he might never die. "If surviving assassination were an Olympic event, I would win the gold medal,"[93] Castro once joked. What Castro could not survive was gastrointestinal bleeding that left him too weak to rule.

Raúl Castro, right, who played a critical role in his brother Fidel's regime beginning with their days as rebel insurgents in the 1950s, assumed temporary power of Cuba in 2006, after Fidel suffered a health crisis. He was officially elected president by the Cuban parliament in February 2008 after Fidel formally relinquished his office.

Except for a brief medical statement, the world learned little about Castro's health for the next year. Some people speculated Castro had a more serious illness, such as cancer, and as months went by without a public appearance, other people began to believe he was dead. On June 5, 2007, however, Castro emerged from his long seclusion by giving a brief television interview. He looked weak and was rarely seen in public after that.

As 2008 began without Castro resuming power, Cubans and people in other countries wondered whether he would ever again be strong enough to govern Cuba. On February 19, the eighty-one-year-old Castro announced he was stepping down as president because he was no longer fit enough to serve his country. "It would be a betrayal to my conscience to accept a responsibility requiring more mobility and dedication than I am physically able to offer,"[94] Castro wrote in a letter published in *Granma*.

Castro and Castro

Six days after Castro's announcement, Cuba's National Assembly elected Raúl president to succeed his brother. Raúl said he was taking the position knowing that "as far as the commander in chief is concerned there is only one. Fidel is Fidel."[95] He promised he would consult with his older brother on any decisions he made. His statement demoralized many Cubans who had hoped Raúl would make changes to improve life, and many people believed that Fidel would continue to wield the real power in Cuba.

In just a few months, however, the seventy-six-year-old Raúl began to surprise people with small but significant changes in how Cubans lived. He lifted bans that prohibited average people from buying computers, DVD players, and cellular telephones. Cuba's ban on such products had been partially due to energy shortages but also to keep people from using the Internet and other communications devices to work against the government. Many people, however, did not have enough money to buy computers or cell phones because they made so little money; the average salary was about twenty dollars a month. But Raúl, who had pushed tourism as a way to counter the economic hardship of the Special Period, removed government-imposed ceilings on wages to create more incentives for people to work hard. He also expanded private farming and gave farmers more freedom in choosing what to grow.

Although Fidel is no longer Cuba's top leader, he made sure he would not be forgotten by writing a series of articles for *Granma* titled *Reflections of Fidel*. In one titled "Don't Make Concessions to Enemy Ideology," Fidel asked Cubans to think deeply about changes his brother was making. Although he seemed to disagree with the new freedoms, he did not condemn them. Dan Erikson, a senior associate at the Inter-American Dialogue in Washington, D.C., said Raúl faced a difficult task in succeeding his brother: "Does he disappoint Fidel or does he disappoint the Cuban people? The reality is that the legitimacy of his government rests on pleasing Cubans but not straying too far from Fidel."[96] One of the Cubans that Raúl made happy with his initial steps to loosen government control was his daughter Mariela, who believes in expanding individual freedoms.

Mariela, a married mother of three children, heads the National Center for Sexual Education. In May 2008, her agency held a week-long festival in Havana and six of Cuba's fourteen provinces to increase public awareness about gay rights, a big change from the harsh treatment gay people received when Cuba first turned Communist. Mariela has also advocated allowing Cubans to travel freely and to leave if they want. Travel outside of Cuba is heavily restricted, and people who try to defect to the United States are punished if they are caught.

Perhaps the most difficult problem facing Castro's successor is the island's relationship with the United States. When Castro resigned as president he still hated the United States, a feeling that was reciprocated by his old Cold War foe. U.S. officials in 2008 continued to maintain the decades-old economic embargo that has weakened Cuba financially and still prohibits citizens from visiting the island. Raúl is believed to be more agreeable to reestablishing relations with the United States, primarily because it could strengthen the Cuban economy. He would have to directly defy his brother to do that, however. Castro has always been proud of his opposition to Cuba's bigger, much more powerful neighbor, which he likes to refer to as the "mighty empire."

How Will History Judge Castro?

When Luiz Inácio Lula da Silva, president of Brazil, heard that Castro was stepping down as Cuba's top leader, he declared that "Fidel is the only living myth in the history of humanity. The myth lives on."[97] Long after Fidel dies, however, historians will evaluate his life, his accomplishments, and any myths associated with him—one is that the Central Intelligence Agency once proposed using an exploding cigar to assassinate Castro—to determine the impact he made on Cuba and the rest of the world.

When Castro was defending himself in 1953 on charges of attacking the Moncada Barracks, he declared that history would absolve him from any crimes because he had done the right thing by trying to overthrow Batista. But in *Fidel Castro: My Life*, his oral autobiography, which was published in 2006, Castro wrote that he does not care about such judgments: "That's something it's not worthwhile worrying about. You know why? Because this mankind has made so many mistakes, there've been so many stupidities, that if [mankind] manages to survive—which is yet to be seen—if it manages to survive, in 100 years people will look back on us as tribes of barbarians and uncivilized cavemen who aren't worth remembering."[98]

Castro Is on the Losing Side of History

[Castro] pursued egalitarian ideals of free health care, housing and education, while jailing and terrorizing those who disagreed with him. He played world politics with the skill of a grandmaster, but ended up on the losing side of history, with his power confined to a small and bankrupt nation.

José de Córdoba, "Castro Embodies Contradictions of a Movement," *Wall Street Journal*, February 20, 2008, p. A11.

Introduction: Fidel Castro: A Cold War Survivor

1. Quoted in Georgie Anne Geyer, *Guerrilla Prince: The Untold Story of Fidel Castro*. Boston: Little, Brown, 1991, p. 207.
2. Quoted in Fidel Castro, "Message from the Commander in Chief," *Daily Granma*, February 19, 2008. http://www.gran-ma.cubaweb.cu/2008/02/19/nacional/artic10.html.
3. Quoted in Héctor Tobar, "Castro's Reign Changed the Face of the Region," *Los Angeles Times*, February 23, 2008, p. 1.
4. Quoted in Philip Sherwell, "He Would Never Look You in the Eye," *Sunday Telegraph* (London), February 24, 2008, p. 22.
5. Quoted in Philip Sherwell, "He Would Never Look You in the Eye," p. 22.

Chapter 1: Growing Up Wealthy but Rebellious

6. Quoted in Tad Szulc, *Fidel: A Critical Portrait*. New York: William Morrow, 1986, p. 117.
7. Quoted in Volker Skierka, *Fidel Castro: A Biography*. Cambridge, UK: Polity, 2004, p. 6.
8. Quoted in Carlos Franqui, *Diary of the Cuban Revolution*. New York: Viking, 1980, p. 2.
9. Fidel Castro and Ignacio Ramonet, *Fidel Castro: My Life*. New York: Scribner, 2008, p. 74.
10. Quoted in Szulc, *Fidel*, p. 115.
11. Quoted in Skierka, *Fidel Castro*, p. 20.
12. Quoted in Nathaniel Weyl, *Red Star over Cuba: The Russian Assault on the Western Hemisphere*. New York: Devin-Adair, 1961, p. 42.

13. Quoted in Franqui, *Diary of the Cuban Revolution*, p. 1.
14. Quoted in Skierka, *Fidel Castro*, p. 25.
15. Quoted in Weyl, *Red Star over Cuba*, p. 63.
16. Quoted in Szulc, *Fidel*, p. 154.
17. Castro and Ramonet, *Fidel Castro*, p. 98.
18. Quoted in Skierka, *Fidel Castro*, p. 27.
19. Quoted in Geyer, *Guerrilla Prince*, p. 74.
20. Quoted in Geyer, *Guerrilla Prince*, p. 51.

Chapter 2: Castro's Failed Revolution

21. Quoted in Herbert L. Matthews, *Fidel Castro*. New York: Simon and Schuster, 1969, p. 64.
22. Quoted in Szulc, *Fidel*, p. 196.
23. Quoted in Geyer, *Guerrilla Prince*, p. 95.
24. Quoted in Jerry A. Sierra, "Fulgencio Batista. He Was Called El Hombre, 'The Man,' and for Three Decades He Ruled Cuba." http://www.historyofcuba.com/history/batista.html.
25. Quoted in Skierka, *Fidel Castro*, p. 32.
26. Quoted in Szulc, *Fidel*, p. 223.
27. Castro and Ramonet, *Fidel Castro*, p. 106.
28. Quoted in Szulc, *Fidel*, p. 216.
29. Quoted in Robert E. Quirk, *Fidel Castro*. New York: Norton, 1993, p. 46.
30. Quoted in Franqui, *Diary of the Cuban Revolution*, p. 54.
31. Quoted in Geyer, *Guerrilla Prince*, p. 116.
32. Castro and Ramonet, *Fidel Castro*, p. 129.
33. Quoted in Franqui, *Diary of the Cuban Revolution*, p. 61.
34. Quoted in Skierka, *Fidel Castro*, p. 35.
35. Quoted in Szulc, *Fidel*, p. 276.
36. Fidel Castro, "History Will Absolve Me," excerpts from his own defense, delivered at his trial, October 16, 1953. http://social.chass.ncsu.edu/slatta/hi216/documents/dabsolve.html.
37. Quoted in Matthews, *Fidel Castro*, p. 63.

Chapter 3: Castro Invades Cuba

38. Castro, "History Will Absolve Me."
39. Quoted in Geyer, *Guerrilla Prince*, p. 42.
40. Quoted in Quirk, *Fidel Castro*, p. 61.
41. Quoted in Skierka, *Fidel Castro*, p. 37.
42. Quoted in Szulc, *Fidel*, p. 321.
43. Quoted in Peter G. Bourne, *Fidel*. New York: Dodd, Mead, 1986, p. 111.
44. Quoted in Geyer, *Guerrilla Prince*, p. 140.
45. Quoted in I. Lavretsky, *Ernesto Che Guevara*. Moscow: Progress Press, 1976. www.chehasta.narod.ru/1stpart.html.
46. Quoted in Skierka, *Fidel Castro*, p. 42.
47. Castro and Ramonet, *Fidel Castro*, p. 176.
48. Quoted in Szulc, *Fidel*, p. 364.
49. Quoted in Franqui, *Diary of the Cuban Revolution*, p. 124.
50. Quoted in Skierka, *Fidel Castro*, p. 48.
51. Quoted in Franqui, *Diary of the Cuban Revolution*, p. 125.
52. Castro and Ramonet, *Fidel Castro*, p. 185.
53. Quoted in Franqui, *Diary of the Cuban Revolution*, p. 132.

Chapter 4: Castro Brings Revolution to Cuba

54. Herbert L. Matthews, "Cuban Rebel Is Visited in Hideout, Castro Is Still Alive and Still Fighting in Mountains," *New York Times*, February 24, 1957, p. 1.
55. Castro and Ramonet, *Fidel Castro*, p. 185.
56. Herbert L. Matthews, "Cuban Rebel Is Visited in Hideout," p. 1.
57. Sierra Maestra Manifesto (July 12, 1957). Indiana University Latin American Studies Internet Site. www.latinamerican studies.org/cuban-rebels/manifesto.html.
58. Quoted in Jon Lee Anderson, *Che Guevara: A Revolutionary Life*. New York: Grove, p. 251.
59. Quoted in Skierka, *Fidel Castro*, p. 61.
60. Quoted in Szulc, *Fidel*, p. 459.

61. Quoted in Geyer, *Guerrilla Prince*, p. 205.
62. Quoted in Skierka, *Fidel Castro*, p. 76.
63. Castro and Ramonet, *Fidel Castro*, p. 220.
64. Quoted in Skierka, *Fidel Castro*, p. 77.
65. Quoted in Ed Cony, "A Chat on a Train: Castro Describes His Plans for Cuba," *Wall Street Journal*, April 22, 1959, p. 1.
66. Quoted in Quirk, *Fidel Castro*, p. 296.
67. Quoted in Geyer, *Guerrilla Prince*, p. 258.

Chapter 5: Castro Versus the United States

68. Quoted in Sebastian Balfour, *Castro*. New York: Longman, 1990, p. 64.
69. Quoted in George Gedda, "Diplomat Recalls Cuba Break in 1961," January 1, 2001. http://www.fiu.edu/~fcf/diplobrk1101.html.
70. Quoted in John F. Kennedy inaugural address, January 20, 1961. www.americanrhetoric.com/speeches/jfkinaugural.html.
71. Castro Announces Victory. Castro Speech Data Base. Latin American Network Information Center–LANIC. April 20, 1961. http://www1.lanic.utexas.edu/project/castro/db/1961/19610420.html.
72. Quoted in Quirk, *Fidel Castro*, p. 395.
73. Quoted in Skierka, *Fidel Castro*, p. 128.
74. Quoted in Sidney C. Moody Jr., ed., *Triumph and Tragedy: The Story of the Kennedys*. New York: Western Printing and Lithographic, 1968, p. 178.
75. Quoted in James G. Blight and Philip Brenner, *Sad and Luminous Days: Cuba's Struggle with the Superpowers After the Missile Crisis*. Lanham, MD: Rowman & Littlefield, 2002, p. 32.
76. Quoted in Barbara Harrison and Daniel Terris, *A Twilight Struggle: The Life of John Fitzgerald Kennedy*. New York: Lothrop, Lee & Shepard, 1992, p. 118.
77. Quoted in Blight and Brenner, *Sad and Luminous Days*, p. 25.

78. Quoted in Herbert L. Matthews, "Cuba: Eight Years of Revolution," *New York Times*, January 2, 1967, p. 1.
79. Quoted in Balfour, *Castro*, p. 87.
80. Quoted in Charles Lane, "Castro Bucks the Tide," *Newsweek*, April 30, 1990, p. 35.
81. Quoted in "The Bitter Family," *Time*, July 10, 1964. http://www.time.com/time/magazine/article/0,9171,871241-1,00.html.

Chapter 6: Castro and Communism Fade in Cuba

82. Quoted in Georgie Anne Geyer, "The Unexpected Lives of Fidel Castro," *World & I*, May 2001, p. 265.
83. Quoted in Linda Robinsion, "Castro's New Revolution," *U.S. News & World Report*, June 24, 1991, p. 38.
84. Quoted in Skierka, *Fidel Castro*, p. 365.
85. Quoted in Derek Maul, "A Peter Pan Doctor," *Brandon [FL] News & Tribune*, April 5, 2008, p. 1.
86. Quoted in Joseph Contreras, "Island of Failed Promises," *Newsweek*, March 3, 2008, p. 31.
87. Quoted in Mark Bowman, "Opener Special for Peña, Escobar. Childhood Pals Contrast Life in Cuba to Experience with Braves," MLB.com, April 1, 2008. http://mlb.mlb.com/news/article.jsp?ymd=20080401&content_id=2478448&vkey=news_mlb&fext=.jsp&c_id=mlb.
88. Castro and Ramonet, *Fidel Castro*, p. 348.
89. Quoted in Thomas C. Tobin, "On the Air: Voice of an Exiled Daughter," *St. Petersburg (FL) Times*, March 18, 2002. http://www.sptimes.com/2002/03/18/news_pf/State/On_the_air__Voice_of_.shtml.
90. Quoted in Héctor Tobar, "Castro's Latin American Legacy," *Los Angeles Times*, February 23, 2008. http://articles.latimes.com/2008/feb/23/world/fg-latin23.
91. Quoted in Juan O. Tamayo, "Fidel's Private Life with His Wife and Sons Is So Secret That Even the CIA Is Left to Wonder,"

Miami Herald, October 8, 2000. http://www.latinamerican-studies.org/fidel/castro-family.html.

92. Quoted in Jon Lee Anderson, "The Power of Gabriel García Márquez," *New Yorker*, September 27, 1999. http://www.themodernword.com/gabo/gabo_power.html.

93. Quoted in "A Life of Avoiding Assassination Plots," *Press and Journal* (Aberdeen, Scotland), February 20, 2008, p. 16.

94. Quoted in Fidel Castro, "Message from the Commander in Chief," www.granma.cubaweb.cu/2008/02/19/nacional/artic10.html.

95. Quoted in Miguel Bustillo and Carol J. Williams, "Cuba Stays the Course," *Milwaukee Journal Sentinel*, February 25, 2008, p. A3.

96. Quoted in Tim Padgett, "Castro Family Values: Fidel vs. Raul," *Time*, April 17, 2008, www.time.com/time/world/article/0,8599,1732103,00.html.

97. Quoted in Juan Forero, "The Two Paths of Castro's Legacy in Latin America," *Washington Post*, February 20, 2008, p. A10.

98. Castro and Ramonet, *Fidel Castro*, p. 589.

Important Dates

August 13, 1926

Fidel Alejandro Castro Ruz is born.

April 9, 1948

Castro participates in violent protests in Bogotá, Colombia, after liberal leader Jorge Eliécer Gaitán is shot to death.

October 12, 1948

Castro marries Mirta Díaz-Balart.

September 1950

Castro graduates from Havana University and opens a law practice in Havana.

March 10, 1952

Fulgencio Batista seizes power in Cuba through a military coup d'état.

July 26, 1953

Castro's attack on Moncada Barracks fails.

October 16, 1953

Castro gives his final argument in his trial for treason—"La Historia me absolvera" (History Will Absolve Me)—and is convicted and sentenced to fifteen years in prison.

May 15, 1955

Castro is freed after serving less than two years in prison.

December 2, 1956

Castro and eighty-one men invade Cuba in their attempt to oust Batista.

January 1, 1959

Batista flees Cuba, giving Castro victory in the Cuban Revolution; seven days later Castro enters Havana in triumph.

January 3, 1961

The United States ends diplomatic relations with Cuba.

April 17, 1961

The Bay of Pigs invasion by Cuban exiles begins.

October 1962

The Cuban Missile Crisis, the most dangerous incident of the Cold War, takes place.

June 1964

Juanita Castro, Fidel's sister, defects to join tens of thousands of other Cuban exiles in the United States.

1991

The Union of Soviet Socialist Republics disbands.

July 31, 2006

An ill Castro appoints his brother Raúl to handle the duties of president.

February 19, 2008

Castro declines to run again for president, ending nearly a half-century reign as Cuba's most powerful leader.

For More Information

Books

Fidel Castro, *Fidel: My Early Years*. New York: Ocean Press, 2005. An autobiography of Castro's childhood through his victory in the Cuban Revolution.

Leycester Coltman, *The Real Fidel Castro*. New Haven, CT: Yale University Press, 2005. This biography delves into Castro's personal as well as public life.

Clive Foss, *Fidel Castro*. Charleston, SC: History Press, 2006. A solid biography of Castro.

Richard Platt, *Fidel Castro*. Austin, TX: Raintree Steck-Vaughn, 2003. A biography of Fidel Castro for the younger reader.

Michael V. Uschan, *The Cold War: Political Leaders*. Detroit: Lucent Books, 2003. Biographies of Fidel Castro and other political figures during the Cold War.

Web Sites

American Experience: Fidel Castro (http://www.pbs.org/wgbh/amex/castro/). Public Broadcasting System. Background, interviews with experts, pictures, and maps about Fidel Castro and his life.

Castro Speech Database (http://lanic.utexas.edu/la/cb/cuba/castro.html). This database by the University of Texas includes speeches, interviews, and other text sources on Fidel Castro from 1959 to 1996.

CIA World Factbook (https://www.cia.gov/library/ publications/the-world-factbook/geos/cu.html). This Internet site by the Central Intelligence Agency features a map and brief descriptions of the geography, economy, government, and people of Cuba.

Cuba—National Geographic (www3.nationalgeographic.com/places/countries/country_cuba.html). Cuba facts, information and history, travel videos, flags, photos from *National Geographic* magazine.

The Cuban Revolution (1952–1958) (http://www .latinamericanstudies.org/cuban-revolution.html). Historian Antonio de la Cova created this Internet site on Latin American countries, including Cuba. This section has documents, photographs, and other background information on the Cuban Revolution.

Fidel Castro (http://history1900s.about.com/od/fidelcastro/ Fidel_Castro.html). History About.com. A biography of Fidel Castro and links to other sites about the Cuban leader.

History of Cuba (www.historyofcuba.com/main/contents.html). An Internet site on Cuban history that includes copies of speeches and biographical information on Fidel Castro.

Picture Credits

About the Author

Michael V. Uschan has written more than sixty books, including *Life of an American Soldier in Iraq*, for which he won the 2005 Council for Wisconsin Writers Juvenile Nonfiction Award. It was the second time he had won the award. Uschan began his career as a writer and editor with United Press International, a wire service that provides stories to newspapers, radio, and television. Journalism is sometimes called "history in a hurry," and Uschan considers writing history books a natural extension of the skills he developed in his many years as a journalist. He and his wife, Barbara, reside in the Milwaukee suburb of Franklin, Wisconsin.